COACHING SOCCER
6 TO 10 YEAR OLDS
PLANNING SOCCER PRACTICES FOR
6 TO 7 AND 8 TO 10 YEAR OLD PLAYERS

by Giuliano Rusca

Library of Congress Cataloging - in - Publication Data

Rusca, Giuliano
Coaching Soccer 6 to 10 Year Olds

ISBN No. 1-890946-31-1
Library of Congress Cataloging Number 99-74794
Copyright © July 1999

Art Direction and Graphic Design
Kimberly N. Bender
Roberto Santandrea

Editing and Proofing
Bryan R. Beaver

Translated from Italian
Maura Modanesi

Editorial Coordination
Marco Marchel

Technical Coordination
Ferretto Ferretti

Printed by
DATA REPRODUCTIONS
Auburn, Michigan

REEDSWAIN INC.
612 Pughtown Road • Spring City, Pennsylvania 19475
1-800-331-5191 • www.reedswain.com

FOREWORD

The main task of any coach involved in youth soccer is to help his players learn and improve basic technical skills in a very gradual manner, using special coaching methods and contents that are appropriate to the age of the athletes with whom he is dealing.

The coach should first be able to enhance and successfully exploit the player's personal skills and help him acquire and improve all those technical and tactical movements he still cannot make perfectly and easily. Moreover, it is fundamental to understand that for a coach to successfully carry out his activity - coaching soccer - he obviously needs to be an educator first. As a matter of fact, when you are dealing with 6 to 10 year old players you first need to convey and teach them human values, in addition to coaching basic technical skills.

Giuliano Rusca - a youth soccer coach I have known for many years - has been able to perfectly and successfully combine the two main functions that specifically characterize this 'profession', that is the role of educator and that of coach.

Giuliano has clearly understood that soccer activity at this level and age is first of all play and pleasure and should therefore be coached and experienced in this particular light.

Furthermore, he has also understood that exasperated use of tactics is practically useless when trying to help inexperienced players improve their skills; it even deprives players of their personal imagination and creativeness. When soccer is lacking both creativeness and imagination, it inevitably loses those features that made, are making and will always make it such a popular, fascinating and exciting sport.

He clearly expresses his thoughts and innovative ideas in this book that I would define 'a great proof and display of enthusiasm' towards coaching soccer that is now becoming increasingly difficult and demanding and is considered increasingly important for the growth of the athlete of course, but also and specifically for the personal maturation of the human being.

I do hope all the coaches educators will further enjoy their job and consider it in a different light after reading this practical handbook. In conclusion, I would like to underline once again that a soccer player can grow and mature only through the great enthusiasm, the strong will and the passion that his coach can personally apply to his job and convey to his athletes.

Enjoy your coaching!

Mario Mereghetti
Technical manager of the
Youth Section at Club F.C.
INTER MILAN

INTRODUCTION

'I owe a great deal to soccer for everything I know today'

Camus

Particularly receptive to all those aspects that may introduce significant innovations in the process of both coaching and learning soccer, I found it important and helpful to offer my new suggestions to all my fellow coaches who are particularly sensitive to changes and innovative solutions and consequently consider a book as a valid support to their coaching.

A book should offer:

- important directions and goals
- clearly explained methods and solutions
- the possibility to check and verify the goals that have been achieved at last and the way they have been reached, while also adjusting or modifying original plans, if necessary.

Through my personal suggestions included in this book I would like to lay the bases for a new coaching method. A truly innovative method that is completely detached from the criteria that are typical of early coaching, but also satisfies our players' need and strong desire to play soccer at the same time.

A modern coaching method where the relationship between the coach and the player is not traditionally characterized by the superiority of the adult prevailing over the player's immaturity, but is based on a direct approach of an 'eternally ludic and highly sensitive person' to all the problems of the players playing soccer.

This work is a successful combination of both 'themes' and 'communication' allowing the readers to better understand an innovative method they may use to coach and educate young soccer players.

This book is completely focused on youth soccer, always considering that any player between the age of 6 to 10 typically has a burning curiosity to know and learn everything possible and a highly developed learning capacity that naturally diminishes as time goes by.

Anybody who is still willing and able 'to play' may potentially appreciate and use my personal suggestions.

YOUTH SOCCER: AN EDUCATIONAL AND FORMATIVE ROLE FOR LONG TERM RESULTS

"A journalist once asked the German theologian Dorothee Solle: "How would you explain to a player what happiness is?" "I would not try to explain it verbally", she answered, "I would simply give him a ball and let him play".

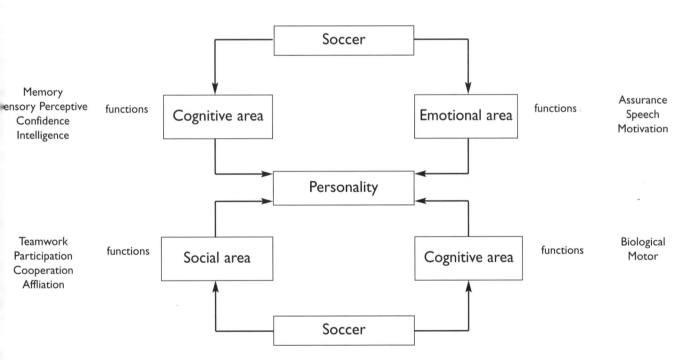

Youth soccer at any level or age group obviously has a mainly educational and formative task. Coaches should first of all focus their attention on the complete development of all the various components of their young athletes' personality.

The human being can grow and mature only if his cognitive, social, emotional and physical functions are constantly enhanced and enriched.

Any coaching or educational activity should primarily focus on the player.

As a matter of fact, in youth soccer great attention should be given to the educational component that soccer obviously involves: remember that educating means neither simply coaching nor raising young players, but teaching and promoting human values.

Playing soccer also helps shape the human being in all his personal aspects, thus affecting both inner and external features.

From the external point of view, every player

should be offered the possibility to act by himself, free from set behaviors and orders coming from outside, personally training his body to special abilities, self control and confidence in his own skills and energies.

As far as the inner component is concerned, soccer is an opportunity to enhance one's will.

Furthermore, playing soccer considerably helps teach some moral virtues of critical importance like discipline, respect, honor, self control, humbly accepting defeat, winning with grace and developing friendly relationships with opponents.

I think these are particularly important educational goals that can help young players gradually become better people, as well as better soccer players. This is why adults involved in youth soccer at any level or age group should first play the role of 'educational agents'; all those people working in youth soccer (coaches, assistants, trainers, managers and so forth) should be highly reliable adults who freely and deliberately choose to educate young players regardless of any personal benefit and recompense.

They obviously need to work hard and for a very long period of time if they want to achieve those goals, and the results will only be evident in the long term. Undoubtedly, it is first necessary to understand "what one can do", "how one should suggest something", and "how much one should do".

This innovative coaching and educational process starts at a very early age and specifically concerns 6 to10 year old players. As a matter of fact, the period between the ages of 6 and 10 is extremely critical and particularly important for the maturation and training of the future adult and athlete as well; this is the crucial period when the functional bases and premises for a proper didactic and educational process should be laid.

The main purpose of coaching youth soccer - always referring to the age of 6 to 10 - is to teach and enhance individual motor skills in order to achieve a perfect and ideal motor performance, which obviously results from the complete development and combination of the player's motor capacities, motor skills and individual personality.

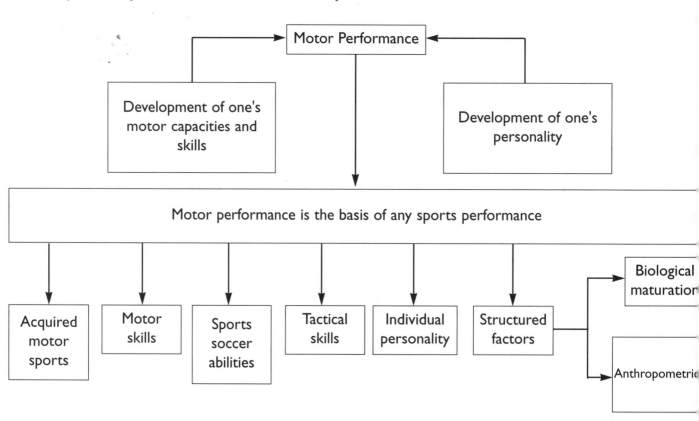

In the following paragraphs, I would like to focus attention on these critical age groups.

Auxology (the branch of medicine dealing with the individual's body growth) clearly explains that several specific phases can be identified in the player's developmental process; this means that a given body weight or a given height on the average generally characterize players at a particular age.

Consequently, it is possible to draw up special tables suggesting the average values of both body weight and height according to the individual's age and sex.

I would like to point out that these tables generally have no absolute value, since every player's growth and development is characterized by their own rhythms and phases; this means that a 10% difference lower or higher than standard values suggested in these tables should not worry, since this is a symptom of neither diseases nor physical disorders.

It is fundamental to underline that many situations of both late and early physical development in players are basically normal at the age of puberty, since this period is characterized by considerably enhanced hormone production.

On the following page, you will find a special table showing both weight and height average values; in addition to carefully identifying and 'classifying' our players, this table gives us the opportunity to accurately assess and follow their growth over the period between the ages of six and ten. Now, I would like to concentrate on the psychological components of this age group.

At the age of six, players begin to attend the elementary school and inevitably need to give up their typically self-centered attitude. From this moment on, they do not only belong to their own families, but they are also part of a peer group and naturally tend to conform to the rules, principles and behavior models of their own communities as time goes by.

This is a period of critical transition and significant changes for the player both from the physical and the psychological point of view. Considerable transformations typically occur in the body of the player and he is often in a precarious state of health, being more susceptible to diseases.

The player's sudden growth obviously upsets his height and weight equilibrium and he gradually begins to develop those traits that will make him look like an adult in the long term.

This period is also characterized by temporary muscular insufficiency. At this point, if the player does not have the opportunity to practice any oriented multilateral motor activity regularly, he may run the risk of losing an important stage in the process of his motor training, a wide motor basis on which he should gradually build his 'pyramid'. This reference to the pyramid is due to the fact that the wider the base of the pyramid, the higher it can grow, thus reaching superior levels of specialization.

Age	Weight/Height	Women	Men
6	weight lbs. height inches/feet	46 3'9"	48 3'10"
6 1/2	weight lbs. height inches/feet	49 3'11"	51 3'11"
7	weight lbs. height inches/feet	52 4'0"	55 4'1"
7 1/2	weight lbs. height inches/feet	52 4'1"	57 4'2"
8	weight lbs. height inches/feet	58 4'2"	60 4'3"
8 1/2	weight lbs. height inches/feet	61 4'3"	63 4'4"
9	weight lbs. height inches/feet	64 4'4"	66 4'5"
9 1/2	weight lbs. height inches/feet	67 4'5"	69 4'6"
10	weight lbs. height inches/feet	70 4'7"	72 4'7"

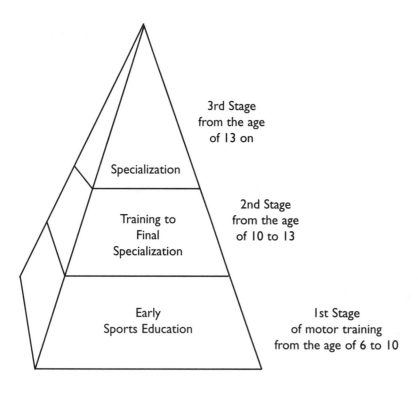

3rd Stage
from the age
of 13 on

Specialization

2nd Stage
from the age
of 10 to 13

Training to
Final
Specialization

Early
Sports Education

1st Stage
of motor training
from the age of 6 to 10

Between the ages of eight and nine, the player generally tends to put on weight, thus restoring the original weight and height balance. He typically gets increasingly interested in the world and people around him and feels a pressing need to get in contact with what he is really interested in.

At this age, the player is usually inclined to seclude himself and take shelter in a peaceful place not to be noticed by others. By contrast, he sometimes adopts an aggressive and hostile attitude towards his own friends, specifically when he wants to draw attention to himself. Moreover, social rules and team games generally become increasingly important in this period. At this age, the player's attention and concentration are still poor; this is why it is advisable for the coach to frequently change the exercises and games he suggests.

At about the age of ten, players begin to enhance their capacity to bear physical effort and the recovery period immediately after strenuous exercise slowly becomes relatively shorter. At this age, it is advisable to introduce a certain amount of exercise involving specific content concerning team tactical skills, since the player is now able to tackle problems from different points of view, gradually overcoming self-centered behaviors and

feeling like an integrating part of a larger group.

Before analyzing all the various purposes of my personal suggestion in detail, I would like to carefully classify all the various elements and features concerning the age, the learning process and the educational method as well.

From the age of 6 to 10

Characteristics typical of the age
- all body systems and organs are still developing
- the capacity to concentrate and pay attention is still very poor
- mainly short term memory
- strong motivation, specifically connected to the need to enjoy oneself
- poor self knowledge

Characteristics of the learning process
- in a global form
- from one's personal experience to abstraction
- this is the best period for the individual to acquire and enhance basic skills and develop connected coordination capacities

Characteristics of the educational method
- immediate motivation and goals that can be easily verified
- every single athlete should be perfectly integrated and involved in the group
- wide range of suggestions, specifically offered in a ludic form
- competition between individual players and groups

THE GOALS OF THIS INNOVATIVE COACHING METHOD

"If there is something we would like to change in a player, we should first consider it carefully and understand whether this is not something we had better change in ourselves."

C.G. Jung - 'The intelligence of personality'

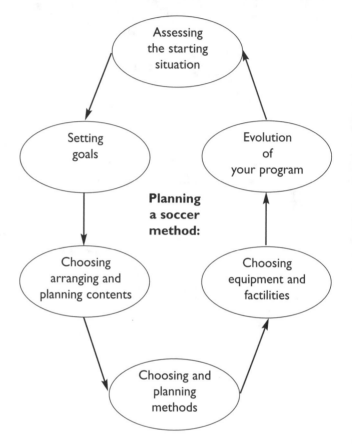

The word 'goal' generally refers to the object of one's efforts, the aim one wants to pursue, the final target one tries to achieve.

For instance, if I state that the main goal for youth soccer teams is *'to coach specific technical and tactical skills peculiar to soccer'*, I'm making a mistake, since this formulation is practically useless. It is too generic, vague and does not offer specific information about all the various motor behaviors that such an activity involves.

A useful goal clearly describes how the athlete will acquire such skills. Setting clear and distinct goals in youth soccer is particularly important in the context of planning specific coaching methods and activities over a period of one year or more. As a matter of fact, while setting special goals it is also possible to identify the final targets, as well as all the various phases and stages of the whole learning process.

In order to accurately set the goals that youth soccer teams should pursue for players between the ages of 6 to 10, it is first of all fundamental to understand what soccer really is at this age. At this particular age, playing soccer is simply a starting point and not an ultimate end, a helpful means to express one's motor capacities that can help enhance the development of one's personality, like many other educational activities in a much wider perspective of variable motions.

It is play that satisfies the above mentioned ludic needs of the player and therefore acts as a 'mediator' of both the learning and socialization processes.

This game can offer a balancing function between the player's energies, personal drives and instincts and the educational needs of the **world of adults**.

In this way, it is possible to lay the necessary bases and premises of a truly innovative method that is aimed at teaching and learning a healthy and positive manner to practice physical exercise, going far beyond the false myth of budding champions and exasperated competition.

The following paragraphs will concentrate on both the general and specific goals of this innovative coaching method, analyzing them in detail. The expression "general purposes" defines the performances that every single player should be able to make at the end of a specific coaching cycle over a period of one or more years.

By contrast, specific goals are definitely more accurate and detailed than general targets.

Characteristics of soccer as a game

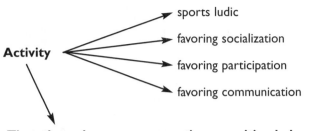

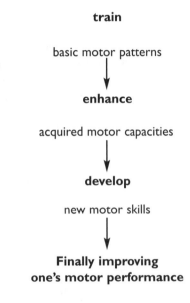

Age	General purpose	Specific purpose
6 to 7 year olds	Acquiring and enhancing basic movements and techniques like running, jumping, rolling on the ground, throwing, catching. On these basic skills will be based the learning of specific abilities in a global form so as to enhance those fundamental coordination skills that play a key role in the choice of the movement one wants to make, in the direction and its control as well.	■ running within marked areas ■ throwing balls of different sizes ■ jumping high and long ■ catching balls of different sizes ■ rolling and diving on the ground ■ dribbling the ball ■ kicking the ball ■ receiving and controlling the ball ■ heading the ball
8 to 9 year olds	Modifying, adjusting, improving, enhancing and combining all those skills and elements that have slowly been acquired in the previous phases, while also gradually shifting from general coordination to specific coordination.	■ throwing the ball ■ dribbling the ball ■ kicking the ball ■ controlling the ball ■ running and throwing the ball ■ running and kicking the ball ■ running and controlling the ball ■ running and heading the ball ■ dribbling and kicking the ball ■ controlling and kicking the ball ■ controlling and dribbling the ball ■ from unconditioned 3 v 3 to 5 v 5
10 year olds	Shifting from specific situations or Preparatory and preliminary games to soccer games involving specific rules and suitable structures.	■ enhancing all the combinations of skills previously acquired ■ challenging and preventing the opponent's offensive action ■ defending the goal and the shooting area ■ regaining possession of the ball ■ maintaining individual ball possession and screening the ball ■ handling 1 v 1 and 2 v 1 situations successfully ■ from unconditioned 5 v 5 to 7 v 7

When the coach has those specific goals clear in his mind, he will certainly be able to plan his coaching activity consistently and clearly, in relation to every single specific goal he wants to achieve.

We thought it advisable to divide the learning process developing in players of this age in three different stages, each one involving the final achievement of some general and specific goals.

The passage from one stage to the following one should take place very gradually, always remembering that players first need to acquire and properly master the contents of the previous phase before dealing with something new. In this way, each stage will obviously lay the bases for the following ones.

THE ROLE OF THE COACH

"Education should be a sort of pleasure in the first years of your life; only in this way will you find it much easier to discover your natural inclinations".

Plato, "The republic"

The first important task of a coach working in youth soccer should be to "examine" and know the players he is dealing with, to accept them for what they really are, without wishing to change them or force them to become those ideal models he would like them to be.

Everybody has his own genetic pool that should be enhanced in the best way possible, with no external pressures or constraints. When the coach has clearly identified the skills and movements that every single player should acquire and improve and has specified which level the player has to start from for the learning process to develop successfully, only at this moment can he plan a suitable learning program in which he can include and direct the activity for his young players.

In practice, the coach should:

❑   choose the best inputs so as to keep the player's attention and stimulate positive replies;
❑   communicate to his players all the learning targets they have to pursue;
❑   make sure of the necessary prerequisites;
❑   choose suitable contents to achieve original goals;
❑   help and direct players with suitable suggestions and questions so as to reinforce correct replies;
❑   plan stimulating situations that are aimed at favoring the transfer of acquired skills;
❑   help players internalize and store the skills they have gradually acquired in their memory.

The coach should realize that the age between six to ten is the critical period when all the functional bases and prerequisites are laid for the individual to properly learn and internalize all those specific motor actions. In the previous paragraphs, we have pointed out that basic motor development is the key element and the main prerequisite of the whole technical development that naturally follows.

While giving his soccer "lessons" (in fact, we cannot speak of training sessions, since they are mainly educational and motor ludic suggestions at this age), the coach should clearly and accurately explain all the games and exercises he is suggesting and then let his players try those movements by themselves. Only at the end can he verify if they have acquired those skills through methodical observation and careful analysis of the results.

The soccer lessons - each one lasting no longer than one hour and a half - should be held twice or three times a week, and the groups should not exceed twenty players each. The players should be divided according to their technical level and age so as to form homogeneous groups.

weekly exercise				% of exercise			
age	days	hours	matches	general	specific	specialization	periodization
6-7	2	3	no	100%	-	no	no
8-9	2	3	1	90%	10%	no	no
10	2-3	3-4	1	80%	20%	light	no

The coach in front of the player

Being a coach and educator necessarily involves:

- **Wide knowledge**
  the coach should be highly motivated to know the player as the subject and protagonist of his educational approach
- **Competence**
  the coach should study and constantly refine his coaching methods and techniques, while always operating according to well designed programs and pursuing a mainly educational goal (he should try to understand the mistakes his players are making and not simply correct them so as to prevent them from making the same error over and over again)
- **Predisposition to coach and educate**
  the coach should be able to stimulate interest and attention, communicate, arouse enthusiasm in his players, constantly involve them in any situation, and plan well aimed and highly motivating activities
- **Positive way of living**
  the coach should accept his role of educator positively and optimistically
- **Awareness of being something more**
  cognitive synthesis

The coach plays the role of expert of coaching and education.

There are two distinct methods of coaching and educating. The first method is more traditional, conservative and arbitrary; it is based on authoritative orders and therefore obedience to the superior authority. The coach works by communicating specific information and giving directions that players cannot but accept and apply, pointing out whether they have clearly understood them or not.

This coaching method has a serious handicap: the player can only receive information and orders passively and can learn the best way to act and move only at a very superficial level.

The second coaching and educational method is much more effective. The coach acts as a guide and resource and is very aware that the player plays an active role in this context, since he has all the aptitudes and capacity to learn by himself. This approach is mainly focused on the gradual development of the whole educational process rather than on the learning content and the final outcome. The coach simply offers the means (the games and exercises he suggests) and his active support to his players, while the players apply their will to learn and the act of learning as well.

This method offers two important advantages: the players acquire and internalize a large amount of information and, above all, gradually learn how to think and learn.

PRINCIPLES OF THIS COACHING METHOD

"The principle is the most important element in the whole work"

Plato, The Republic

In the previous paragraphs, we have explained that in this critical period of an individual's life - that is from the age of six to ten - it is advisable to plan and suggest general and diversified activities, having a mainly ludic intent.

The player should be put in a favorable condition to play while moving; motion should be experienced in all its different forms, manners and performances so that the player's natural need to move is fully satisfied.

Consequently, the main role of youth coaches is not to train players but to help them become aware of what they are doing. I am firmly convinced that soccer cannot be suggested in its whole complex nature to players of this age; this means that for inexperienced players to positively approach this sport, soccer technique should be highly simplified, but without its real nature being altered completely.

The coaching and educational process should gradually develop from simple to increasingly complex things, from the known to the unknown. Our activity should be directly connected to the movement from the overall reality to the specific situation, from the general to the detailed. The player naturally feels a strong need to learn, suggest, and choose and therefore needs somebody or something that can enhance his creative abilities. In particular, the player necessarily needs to satisfy his intense desire to play.

For this activity to be effective in this phase of an individual's life, playing soccer should be highly creative, original and inventive; it should be felt as a means to express one's freedom and must therefore be a game, first and foremost!
Play - the educational means par excellence - should be considered prerequisite, a right, a need that cannot be neglected for players in any youth soccer team, and not a prize to be awarded by pure sense of benevolence.

This innovative coaching method specifically aims at using the ludic activity as an instrument to finally transfer to the player those skills he needs to better play soccer with his teammates.

All the activities we are going to suggest to you in this book will have a mainly ludic nature and will gradually get increasingly difficult; they will all comply with the following principles:
❏ allowing the player to make the same movement in different ways
❏ varying the rhythm and speed of the performance
❏ combining all the skills the player has slowly acquired
❏ changing the messages and information one is conveying to the player by stimulating the use of visual, acoustic, tactile and kinesthetic sensory analyzers
❏ making the same movements while changing the area in which one is moving

Some coaches still believe that letting players play during the training session is one of the easiest ways for them to slacken the reins and relieve their responsibilities. By contrast, I am firmly convinced that playing naturally helps players acquire motor skills while also enhancing their capacities to adapt to new situations.

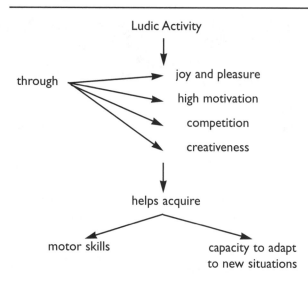

In synthesis:

While the player is playing most of his motor skills are promptly activated and enhanced, so that play inevitably becomes a very helpful support for the biological development and both the learning and socialization processes of the player as well.

Playing should gradually lead to developing specific technique and not vice versa.

In any ludic situation, the coach should constantly help and direct the player, giving him special suggestions on the best way to apply the principles and rules he has previously explained. This approach considerably favors the player's learning process in general and also allows the coach to assess whether the player has clearly understood all the various play mechanisms or not; accurate analysis and evaluation of the level the young player has gradually reached are particularly important since it becomes much easier for the coach to plan the next steps he will take in the context of his innovative coaching approach.

Encouraging and motivating players is key to helping them successfully acquire and develop new play abilities; if motivating athletes also has a purely educational intent, it allows for the adjustment of any player's behavior.

Playing:
❏ is an innate need for the player
❏ helps enhance basic motor capacities in the player
❏ helps create a disinhibited and relaxing atmosphere around the player
❏ improves the player's body image
❏ helps to enhance the player's self-assurance and self-esteem
❏ gradually helps the player to comply with rules through direct experience
❏ regulates the player's attitude towards others
❏ generally makes the job of the coach much easier since it can directly show him the player's behavioral style and patterns.

My intent is to suggest an innovative coaching method that is based on soccer intended as both sport and play; this new approach to soccer specifically highlights the ludic component of sport that best matches with the developmental stages of youth.

Considering the premises, this innovative coaching program is based on the following principles:
❏ the activities specifically designed for this age group should be carried out focusing great attention on play
❏ the coach should avoid suggesting particular play situations involving too large a number of rules or excessively complex contents
❏ the activity should become a means to satisfy the players' needs
❏ the activity should gradually enhance the players' performance
❏ the activity should be planned according to the player's developmental level
❏ the activity should be planned so as to allow the player to gradually shift from basic motor skills to specific abilities
❏ the activity should be suggested so as to involve the whole of each player's personality.

COACHING AND TRAINING MOTOR SKILLS

"In soccer, individual ability is more important than athletic condition and, in many cases, individual ability is the art of turning one's weaknesses into positive virtues."

E. Galeano -
from "Splendors and miseries of soccer"

First of all, I would like to give a definition of motor skill: "Motor skill refers to the individual's capacity to carry out complex, well organized patterns of behavior smoothly and adaptively so as to achieve a well-aimed, predetermined goal through suitable movements".

In sport, technical abilities and movements can be considered real skills and skills can be broadly divided in two different groups: open and closed skills. "Closed skills" generally refer to those motor performances that are carried out in constant environmental conditions and mainly result from both proprioceptive information and inner programs the athlete builds inside himself. On the other hand, "open skills" refer to those motor performances that strictly depend on the changes occurring in the surrounding environment. The degree of predictability of the particular situation where the motor ability is carried out directly determines whether an open or a closed motor skill is used.

The situation of the athlete's performance never changes in some sports, while it is always unpredictable and constantly varies in others.

Soccer is a typical example of a sports discipline where athletes use open motor skills.

For his performance to be really effective, the soccer player should be constantly able to adapt his basic skills and movements (basic techniques) to all the various changeable situations that he faces. In fact, we can easily realize that all the abilities of every single soccer player are harmoniously included in the context of other individuals who position and move in a certain space (the playing field), in a certain time always in relation to an object (the ball), in opposition to another group of individuals (the opposition), who substantially make the same movements to finally achieve the same goal. How does this individual act in the particular moment when he produces a motor skill?

While making movements and therefore carrying out special abilities, the human body typically acts as a computer: by means of a central processor (the brain), the body promptly processes some information in order to bring about specific motor responses (actions) that will be immediately committed to memory and internalized so that they will be easily recalled and used.

This clearly proves that there is a direct connection between sensory perception and motion. The basic model of the information processing mechanism can be schematized as follows:

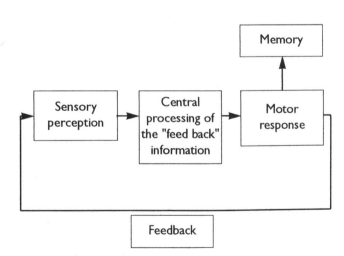

Producing a final, effective movement is possible only after specific developmental stages.

The first phase is characterized by the perception of generalized and undifferentiated stimulus inputs by special sensory analyzers. Analyzers are part of the whole sensory system that, through specific signals conveyed from the outside (acoustic, visual, kinesthetic, olfactory, tactile and gustatory signals), receives, encodes (i.e. converts into another code), forwards and processes information, thus gradually creating memory and sending signals to motor centers. Every single sensory analyzer is made up of its relevant specific receptors, the efferent nerve tracts and the sensory centers, up to the primary projection field of the cerebral cortex. The kinesthetic, tactile, vestibularis, optic and acoustic analyzers are the five sensory analyzers that play a role of crucial importance in the skill learning process.

Both the kinesthetic and vestibularis analyzers belong to the internal regulating circuits, while the three others are included in the external regulating circuits. The five sensory analyzers take part in extremely different percentages in the general process of information on the development of the new skill. They all play a key role in the process of control and regulation of any motor act (ability), since they generally work together and complement each other.

The kinesthetic analyzer perceives the movement; its receptors - called proprioceptors - are present in all muscle groups, joints, tendons and ligaments. Its conducting pathways - superior nerve fibers responsible for transmitting impulses - are much faster than the nerve tracts of the other analyzers: this means that their capacity to conduct impulses is higher. The kinesthetic analyzer plays a key role in the control over the movements the individual is making and over the position of those body segments that are not strictly controlled at the visual level. The vestibularis analyzer (or static dynamic analyzer) is constantly transmitting information concerning the position of one's head in space, and all the positive or negative and angular or straight accelerations the head - and the body as a whole, consequently - receives. The vestibularis analyzer is of great importance for the individual to orientate himself in space.

The optical analyzer plays a role of primary importance in all the various skill learning processes, since its receptors - called teleceptors or distance receptors - allow one to receive those sig-

nals whose transmitter is not in close contact with the receptor, so that light and sound waves act as conducting channels. This means that optical analyzers allow one to receive information not only from one's own movements, but also from the movements of others.

Thanks to this particular characteristic, the optical analyzer plays a role of crucial importance in acquiring and slowly enhancing new skills. In fact, it helps to create a model and it therefore becomes possible to apply to practical performance as useful motor information.

The visual analyzer offers direct information about the starting and final position of a movement and the gradual development of the motor action itself. This analyzer also provides indirect information concerning the position of the body compared to others, the space and all the things around it. Peripheral vision also plays a significant role since it allows us to get information from what is happening beyond our visual attention.

The acoustic analyzer provides us with two different kinds of information: the first type is transmitted through the verbal system, while the other kind of information provided by this analyzer is a combination of all those acoustic signals produced by movement.

The tactile analyzer informs us about all the motor processes developing in close contact with the surrounding environment; information is transmitted through specific receptors present in the skin.

The second phase is the processing of all the information provided by the above-mentioned sensory analyzers; at this stage, the "central processor" (i.e. the brain) interprets all the stimulus inputs that the player is gradually beginning to synthesize. While processing all the information collected, the brain also provides a final solution during this phase.

The following functions are promptly activated:
1. The sensory analyzers convey all the information they have received to the brain. For the brain to use these data in the best way possible, it needs to associate them with the

information that was previously stored in its memory and that is nothing but the final result of all the past experiences of the individual's life.

2. The information that is transmitted into our body is always very complex. For instance, imagine a particular play situation: the information concerning the development of that specific situation in time is combined with that concerning the development of the situation in space and the body as well. This means that the brain first needs to carefully analyze all the data it gets so as to understand and distinguish every single aspect of that particular situation.

3. At this point, the brain starts a synthesis process in order to select and arrange - among all the information it was previously provided - the information it needs to find a suitable solution to the problem it faces.

The third phase is characterized by the motor response that the brain had mentally planned in the previous phase. This phase consists of two different stages that develop as follows:

1. Mental planning: it refers to the capacity to identify and coordinate all the various parts of the body with each other as well as all the space and time elements that are necessary to make movements and take the most suitable postures to carry out the solution the brain has finally found in the processing phase.

2. Motor response: it practically consists of carrying out the mental plan through motor performance. It is possible only if the brain gives special orders to all the various parts of the body that are somehow involved in the movement.

The process developing in a person when he is making a movement cannot stop at this stage, since any motor action his body makes is an inexhaustible source of fresh information. This information is provided both by the movement of the body directly and by the effects that this action has on the surrounding environment, thus creating new possibilities of combination, analysis and synthesis (see the diagram on page 17).

These three important phases should be taken into proper account when planning one's coaching method, since each of them involves specific

goals to be achieved.

For the individual to learn and internalize new motor skills effectively, the following principles must be strictly observed:

1. The player should be perfectly aware of what he is learning.

2. All the exercises and games the coach suggests should allow the player to experience and try various solutions in order to be able to finally choose the most suitable one.

3. Each activity should involve moments of direct and practical experience (the performance), followed by careful analysis and reflection on what has been done.

4. The player should be put in a condition so as to be able to finally assess and understand whether he has made the right choice.

5. The coach should help the player understand that the skill he has gradually acquired can be transferred to soccer, the reason why he has come to the training field.

Accurately planning the activity one is going to suggest is the most important consideration in the whole coaching and educational method. This method is a long process aimed at bringing about some desirable changes in players' behaviors or, better, positively affecting their way of thinking, acting, perceiving and doing.

While drawing up his coaching and educational program, the coach should carefully consider that the player will necessarily pass through special developmental stages to finally acquire new motor skills.

The first phase is that of rough coordination, an early period when the player slowly builds a global pattern of motion: consequently, movements will be poorly coordinated, marginally accurate and highly expensive from the energetic point of view at this stage. The main task of the coach in this phase is to help the player by offering suitable suggestions and a few words of advice and specifically planning activities whose difficulty levels gradually increase according to the athlete's individual abilities. This first phase is also called the "cognitive phase", since the player tries to understand how he has to make that particular movement and what goal he has to achieve. Remember that the young player should be provided with all the information he needs in a very accurate and exhaustive manner in order to acquire and internalize that new skill effectively.

In the second phase - which is better known as refined coordination stage or associative learning phase - the individual tries to reinforce the newly acquired skill so as to make it as spontaneous and automatic as possible through constant practice (continuous reinforcement). This means that the coach should constantly suggest new and different activities always including the newly acquired ability.

When that particular skill has been perfectly internalized and has therefore become automatic, the young athlete can seriously think of how he can apply it in a real situation. This is the phase of variable receptiveness, also called autonomy phase. Only when that particular skill is constantly reinforced and practically applied to real situations can this stage be finally reached. In this period, it is advisable to suggest special situations practically reproducing all the typical space and time features of the game where the ability in question is included. Only in this way can the player gradually learn when and how he should use that skill and make a certain movement.

Different stages in the process to acquire a new motor skill

First Stage	**Cognitive Phase**	The player learns the new motor skill
Second Stage	**Associate Phase**	The player internalizes the new skill
Third Stage	**Autonomy Phase**	The player applies the new skill to a real situation

Ontogeny of the main forms of movements

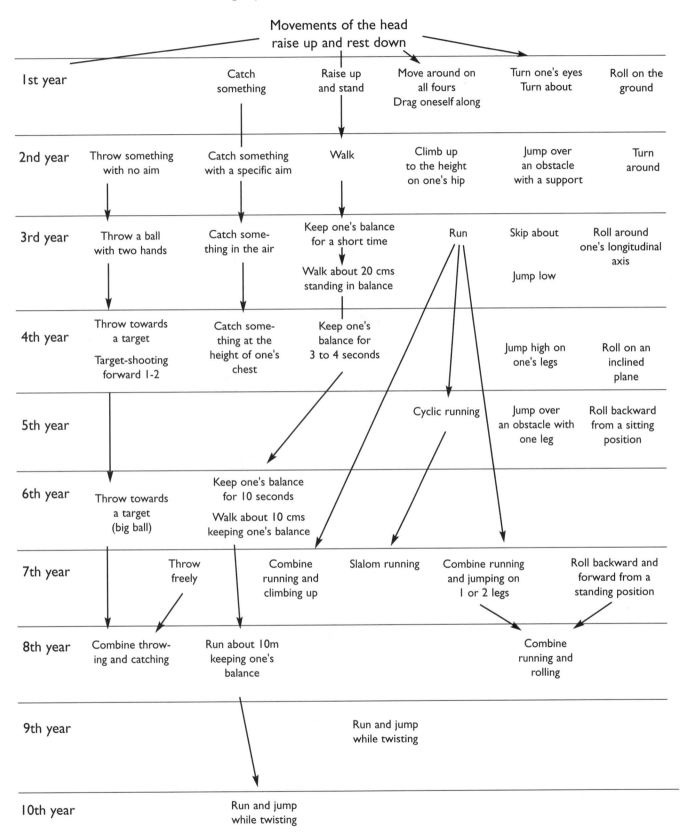

Complete ontogenic development of all basic movements (definite structuring of one's mental image)

Diagram of basic motor skills in relation to age

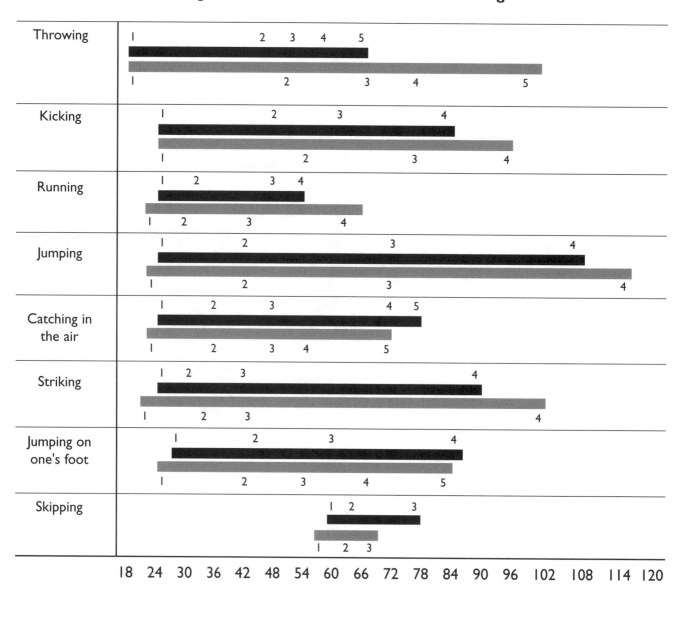

Age (in months)

boys

girls

LEGEND FOR FIELD DIAGRAMS

You can use the following symbols as a reference for all the " graphic explanations" of the drills and games that you will find throughout the book..

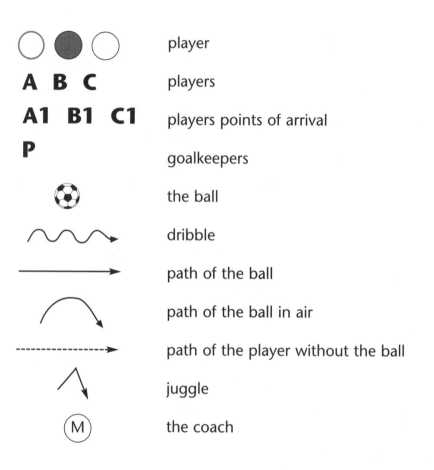

○ ● ○	player
A B C	players
A1 B1 C1	players points of arrival
P	goalkeepers
⚽	the ball
∿∿∿→	dribble
——→	path of the ball
⌢→	path of the ball in air
------→	path of the player without the ball
⋀↓	juggle
Ⓜ	the coach

THE CONTENTS OF THIS COACHING METHOD

The human being can play only when he or she is a human being in the most inclusive sense of the term, and he or she is a complete human being only when he or she is playing.

by Schiller

While I was writing this book I specifically took care to select particular play situations that are suitable for players of this age and can give them pleasure and satisfaction both at a psychological and physical level. For the three different age groups I have tried to suggest three distinct sets of goals so that each set is a prerequisite of the following one. Following this logic, several drills and games - which I have divided into three different levels - are included in this part of the book, specifically focusing on field practice.

At the end of each set of drills it is advisable and helpful to include the information about the results the players have achieved in the three different tests in a summary table (like the example shown on page 23), so as to constantly monitor their performances.

Age group	Final goals	Means
6 to 7 year olds	Learning and reinforcing basic skills and movements like running, jumping, throwing and so forth. These abilities are prerequisite for the individual to acquire and enhance specific skills in a global form	First level Drills
8 to 9 year olds	Enhancing, adjusting, reinforcing and combining all those elements acquired in the previous phase	Second level Drills
10 year olds	Shifting from general skills to specific abilities and movements that are peculiar to soccer	Third level Drills

Summary table for the final goal: drill or game:

Drills and Games / Players	1st test			2nd test			3rd test			4th test			5th test			6th test			7th test			8th test		
	1	2	3	1	2	3	1	2	3	1	2	3	1	2	3	1	2	3	1	2	3	1	2	3
1																								
2																								
3																								
4																								
5																								
6																								
7																								
8																								
9																								
10																								
11																								
12																								
13																								
14																								
15																								
16																								
17																								
18																								
19																								
20																								

FIRST LEVEL DRILLS

This chapter includes all the first level drills and games I have selected that can be used to achieve the first important goal, that is "Enhancing basic motor patterns and learning those skills and movements that are peculiar to soccer".

All the drills I am going to show you in this chapter can be performed either individually or in very small groups of players and pursue the following goals: coaching and acquiring running, jumping, catching, throwing, juggling, dribbling, kicking, controlling and heading skills. First level drills include both exercises without the ball and games that require players to properly handle the ball with both hands and feet.

Two pages offering special directions are dedicated to each drill. One page includes the title of the game, the practical explanation and development of the exercise, both the general and the specific goal the drill is trying to pursue and the field diagram. The other page includes a summary table to catalog the results of the players' performances; this table can help the coach record all the players' scores as well as his coaching notes and personal observations which will allow him to:
- adjust the difficulty level of each drill to the development level of his players' personalities
- plan the themes and contents of the following coaching lessons
- offer players the possibility to make both verbal and diagrammatic remarks about what has been done
- evaluate his educational method.

The drills and games I am going to suggest in the next pages involve a few simple rules that can be easily understood and applied; they are carried out in restricted areas, where all the behaviors and movements useful for the development of that particular activity will directly depend on the players' attention and capacity to carefully listen to the coach's directions.

The final goal of the drill involves the whole group, but the performance of every single player to finally achieve that purpose is definitely more important and prevails over the team work. One player at a time plays the role of protagonist in the game, which implies little cooperation between players.

DRILL 1
Summary table to record and evaluate players' performances

Evaluation / Players	Performance of the wizards		Performance of the free players	
	individual play	distribute tasks	scatter around	move to engaged spaces
1				
2				
3				
4				
5				
6				
7				
8				
9				
10				
11				
12				
13				
14				
15				
16				
17				
18				
19				
20				

DRILL 1

Title:
The wizards

General goal:
Enhancing basic motor patterns

Specific goal:
Running

Explanation:

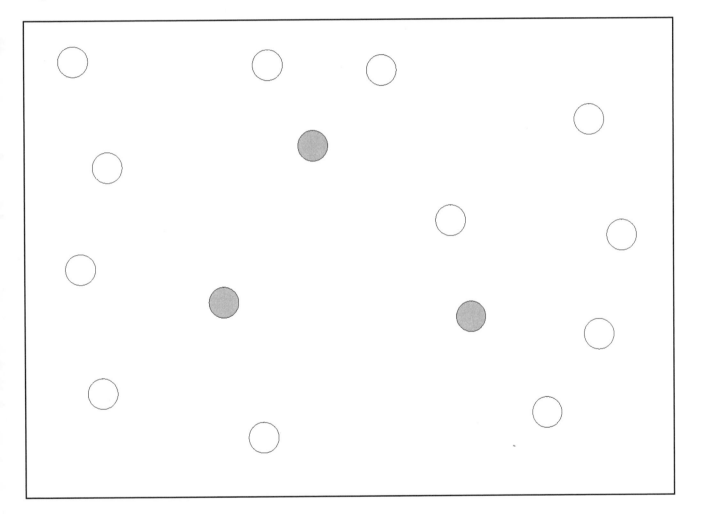

Four players act as wizards ● .
The wizards chase after the free players ○ and try to touch them.
When a free player ○ is touched, he immediately becomes a statue and must stand motionless. He can resume playing only if one of his teammates touches him and sets him free.
When the given time is over, or when all the free players ○ have been touched, the roles of the wizards are assigned to other players.

DRILL 2
Summary table to record and evaluate players' performances

Evaluation / Players	1st Test	2nd Test	3rd Test
	date:	date:	date:
	score:	score:	score:
1			
2			
3			
4			
5			
6			
7			
8			
9			
10			
11			
12			
13			
14			
15			
16			
17			
18			
19			
20			

DRILL 2

Title:
Broad jump into the circle

General goal:
Enhancing basic motor skills

Specific goal:
Jumping skills

Explanation:

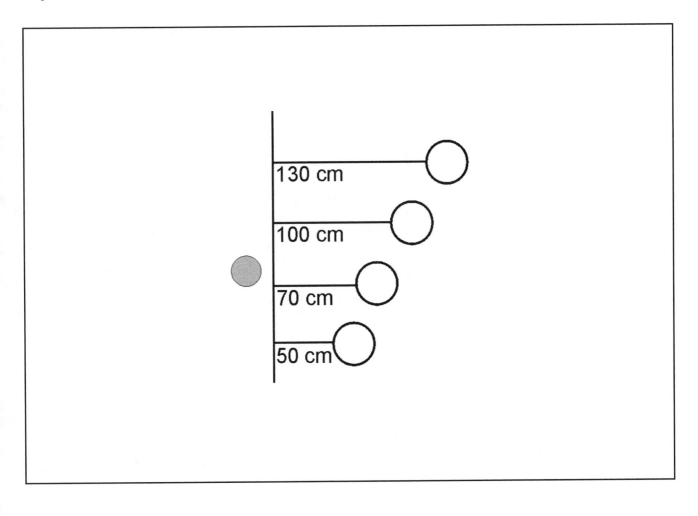

Mark out a straight line on the field; the players are standing along this line and jump with both feet together trying to land in the farthest circle as possible.

Each player can repeat the exercise three times; the performance is valid only if the player jumps into the circle without touching it.

DRILL 3
Summary table to record and evaluate players' performances

Evaluation / Players	1st Test date:		2nd Test date:		3rd Test date:	
	accurate throw	throw with 1-2 hands	accurate throw	throw with 1-2 hands	accurate throw	throw with 1-2 hands
1						
2						
3						
4						
5						
6						
7						
8						
9						
10						
11						
12						
13						
14						
15						
16						
17						
18						
19						
20						

DRILL 3

Title:
Striking the ball

General goal:
Enhancing basic motor skills

Specific goal:
Throwing skills

Explanation:

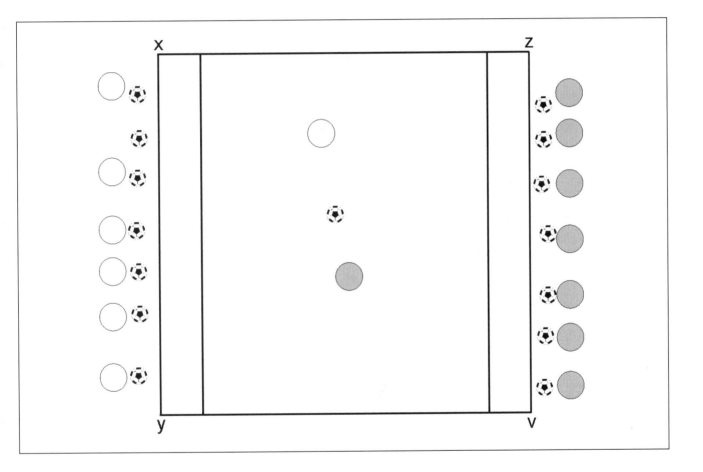

Players ⬤ and ◯ are standing behind the two lines xy and zv respectively, each one holding a ball.
When the coach gives the starting signal, a ball is place in the middle of the playing area.
All the players throw their balls trying to strike the ball lying in the middle so as to make it roll towards the opposite field.
One player on each team moves inside the square to retrieve and return balls to his teammates.
One point is awarded to the team who finally manage to strike the ball and make it cross the opposing line.

DRILL 4
Summary table to record and evaluate players' performances

Evaluation / Players	1st Test	2nd Test	3rd Test
	date:	date:	date:
	score:	score:	score:
1			
2			
3			
4			
5			
6			
7			
8			
9			
10			
11			
12			
13			
14			
15			
16			
17			
18			
19			
20			

DRILL 4

Title:
Take and sprint

General goal:
Enhancing basic motor skills

Specific goal:
Jumping skills

Description:

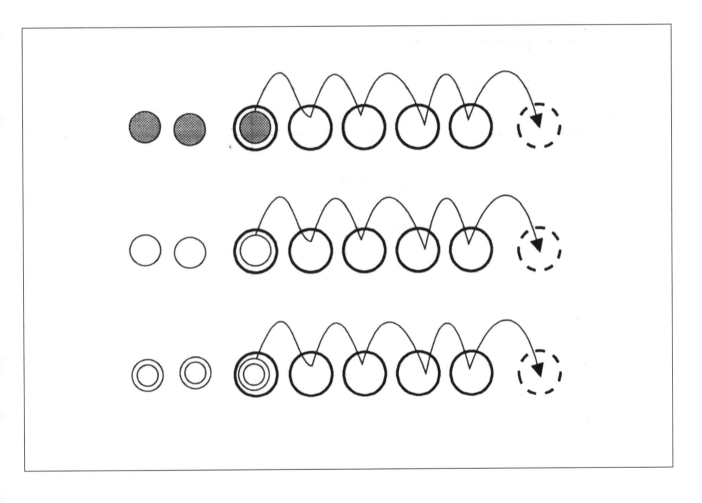

The competition is between two or more teams, each one having four or five hoops.
The hoops are placed close to each other in a straight line in front of the players; when the coach gives the starting signal, the first player of each team jumps into the first hoop, raises it, jumps with both feet together into the following hoops, puts his hoop down at the end of the line and runs back behind his teammates. His teammates perform the same exercise one after the other.
One point is awarded to the player who first manages to complete the circuit and get to the back of his team's line.

DRILL 5
Summary table to record and evaluate players' performances

Evaluation / Players	1st Test date: loses balance		2nd Test date: loses balance		3rd Test date: loses balance	
	yes	no	yes	no	yes	no
1						
2						
3						
4						
5						
6						
7						
8						
9						
10						
11						
12						
13						
14						
15						
16						
17						
18						
19						
20						

DRILL 5

Title:
Crossing the Bricks

General goal:
Enhancing basic motor skills

Specific goal:
Walking while keeping one's balance

Description:

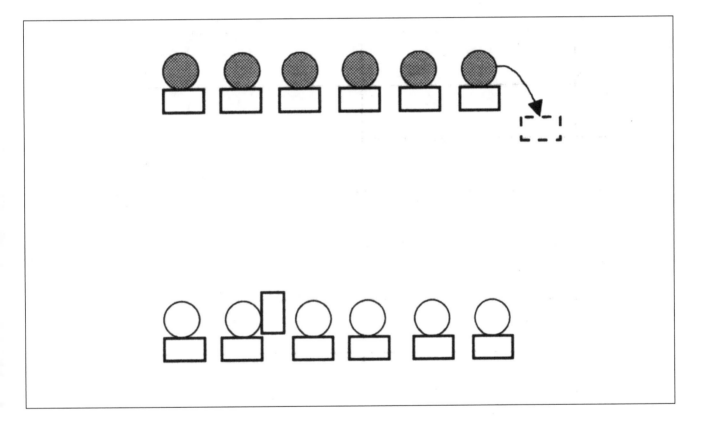

Each team has a certain number of bricks placed in line close to each other.
The players on each team position on the bricks trying to keep their balance.
The last brick lying at the end of the line is picked up, passed from one player to the other and finally placed at the front of the line to allow the team to gradually move forward.
The players cannot put their feet on the ground.
The team who first manages to cross a certain distance wins the competition.

DRILL 6
Summary table to record and evaluate players' performances

Evaluation ⟋ Players	1st Test date: score:	2nd Test date: score:	3rd Test date: score:
1			
2			
3			
4			
5			
6			
7			
8			
9			
10			
11			
12			
13			
14			
15			
16			
17			
18			
19			
20			

DRILL 6

Title:
Get to the opponent's home

General goal:
Enhancing basic motor skills

Specific goal:
Running skills

Description:

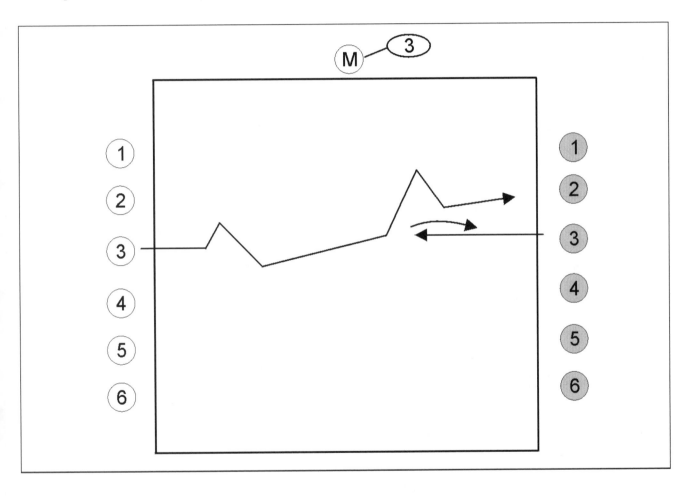

Two teams - the ◯ and the ● made up of six players each. Each player is assigned a number and positions along a straight line in front of his direct opponent.
The ◯ are the defenders while the ● are the attacking players.
When the coach calls a number, the two players with that number sprint out of their home: player ◯ tries to get to ●'s home, preventing his opponent from touching him.
One point is awarded every time the attacking player manages to get to his opponent's home.
The team who can score more points wins the competition.
Switch the roles after three consecutive calls for the attacking players.

DRILL 7
Summary table to record and evaluate players' performances

Evaluation \ Players	1st Test date: accurate throw	1st Test throw with 1-2 hands	2nd Test date: accurate throw	2nd Test throw with 1-2 hands	3rd Test date: accurate throw	3rd Test throw with 1-2 hands
1						
2						
3						
4						
5						
6						
7						
8						
9						
10						
11						
12						
13						
14						
15						
16						
17						
18						
19						
20						

DRILL 7

Title:
Throw and control

General goal:
Enhancing basic motor skills

Specific goal:
Throwing and controlling skills

Description:

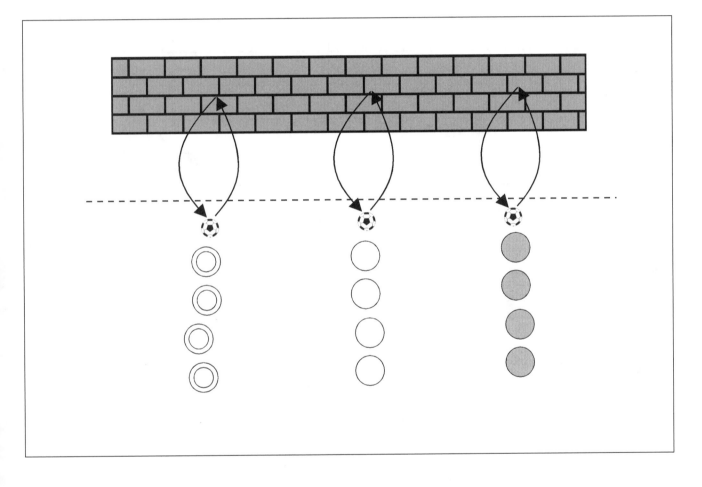

The players are divided in groups of 4 or 5; one ball for each group.
The players are standing in three different lines in front of a wall, they throw the ball against the wall and catch it without letting it bounce on the ground.
After controlling the ball, the first players of the three lines pass the ball to their teammates standing immediately behind them, who do the same thing.
The team who first manages to complete the exercise without dropping any balls wins the game.

DRILL 8
Summary table to record and evaluate players' performances

Evaluation / Players	1st Test	2nd Test	3rd Test
	date:	date:	date:
	score:	score:	score:
1			
2			
3			
4			
5			
6			
7			
8			
9			
10			
11			
12			
13			
14			
15			
16			
17			
18			
19			
20			

DRILL 8

Title:
Throw into the hoop

General goal:
Enhancing basic motor skills

Specific goal:
Throwing the ball

Description:

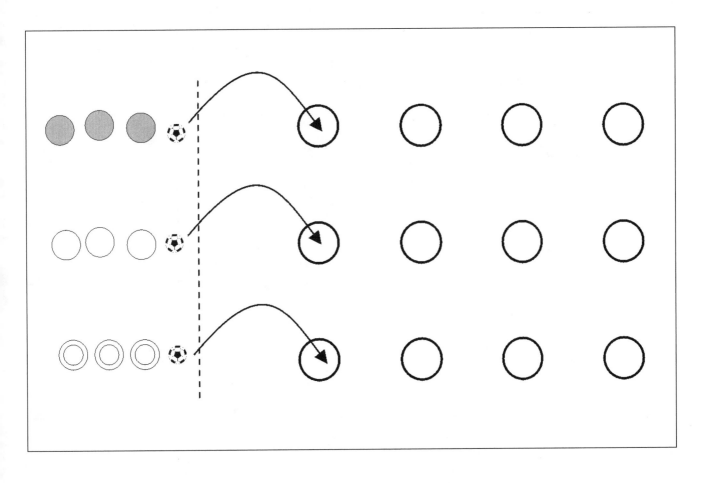

Divide the team into several groups, each player with one ball.
Every player in the group throws the ball trying to land it in the hoop in front of him.
One point is awarded every time a throw lands in the hoop.
Increase the difficulty of the exercise by increasing the distance of the hoops.

DRILL 1
Summary table to record and evaluate players' performances

Evaluation \\ Players	1st Test	2nd Test	3rd Test
	date:	date:	date:
	score:	score:	score:
1			
2			
3			
4			
5			
6			
7			
8			
9			
10			
11			
12			
13			
14			
15			
16			
17			
18			
19			
20			

DRILL 1

Title:
Shoot into the square

General goal:
Enhancing basic motor skills

Specific goal:
Kicking the ball while stimulating one's capacity
to differentiate

Description:

Two players are standing in front of each other in two opposite squares 4 yards wide, at a distance
that can range from 5 to 10 yards.
They kick the ball trying to make it stop in the square of their teammate standing in front of them.
Every player is allowed ten shots into the opposing square.
How many times can he kick the ball in a way so that it stops in the opposing square?

DRILL 2
Summary table to record and evaluate players' performances

Evaluation / Players	1st Test	2nd Test	3rd Test
	date:	date:	date:
	score:	score:	score:
1			
2			
3			
4			
5			
6			
7			
8			
9			
10			
11			
12			
13			
14			
15			
16			
17			
18			
19			
20			

DRILL 2

Title:
Volley shot into the square

General goal:
Enhancing basic motor skills

Specific goal:
Kicking the ball while enhancing one's perception and capacity to differentiate

Description:

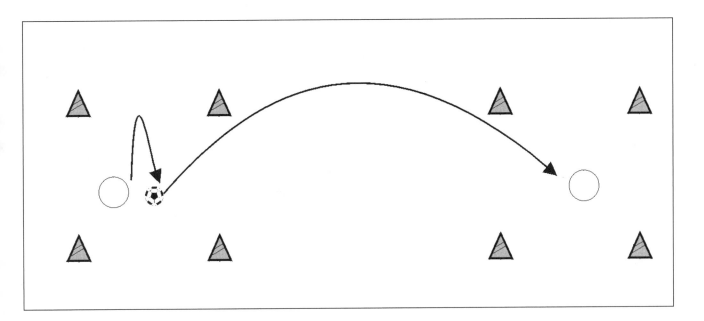

Two players are standing in front of each other in two opposite squares 4 yards wide, at a distance
that can range from 5 to 10 yards in relation to their individual abilities.
The players throw the ball in the air and volley kick it trying to make it bounce in their teammate's
square.
Every player kicks the ball ten times; how many balls bounce directly in the opposite playing area?
One point is awarded every time the ball falls in the opposite square.

DRILL 3
Summary table to record and evaluate players' performances

Evaluation / Players	1st Test date: no. of goals	2nd Test date: no. of goals	3rd Test date: no. of goals
1			
2			
3			
4			
5			
6			
7			
8			
9			
10			
11			
12			
13			
14			
15			
16			
17			
18			
19			
20			

DRILL 3

Title:
Shot on a small sized goal

General goal:
Enhancing basic motor skills

Specific goal:
Accurate shooting

Description:

Two players are standing 10 yards apart behind two opposite small sized goals 2 yards wide; they kick the ball trying to score a goal in the opposing teammate's goal.
Every player is allowed ten shots on goal; how many goals are scored after ten shots?

DRILL 4
Summary table to record and evaluate players' performances

Evaluation / Players	1st Test date:		2nd Test date:		3rd Test date:	
	distance (yards)	no. of goals	distance (yards)	no. of goals	distance (yards)	no. of goals
1						
2						
3						
4						
5						
6						
7						
8						
9						
10						
11						
12						
13						
14						
15						
16						
17						
18						
19						
20						

DRILL 4

Title:
Shooting at a specific target

General goal:
Enhancing basic motor skills

Specific goal:
Accurate and powerful shooting

Description:

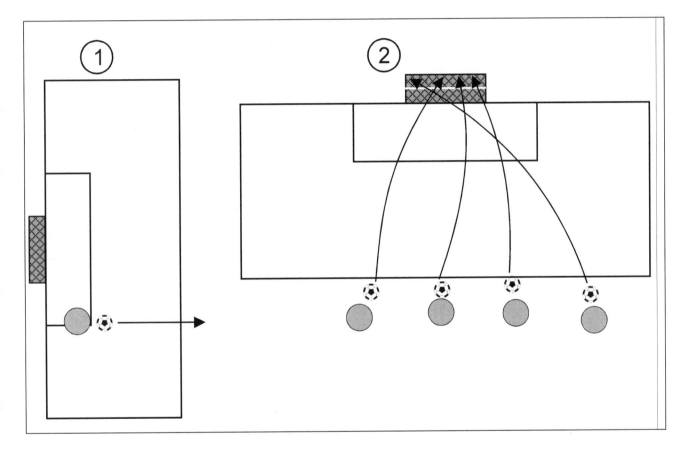

One ball for each player. Ask the players to test all the possible ways to kick the ball with their feet and ask them to shoot at goal using the various techniques. In this way, it is possible to discover:
a. the best way to take a powerful shot on goal, as well as the player who manages to kick the ball the farthest.
b. the best way to take an accurate shot on goal; the players are divided in several teams and position in front of high and low targets.
One point is awarded every time a player can hit the target.

DRILL 5
Summary table to record and evaluate players' performances

Evaluation / Players	1st Test date: score	2nd Test date: score	3rd Test date: score
1			
2			
3			
4			
5			
6			
7			
8			
9			
10			
11			
12			
13			
14			
15			
16			
17			
18			
19			
20			

DRILL 5

Title:
Shooting at a target (between two lines)

General goal:
Enhancing basic motor skills

Specific goal:
Accurate shooting

Description:

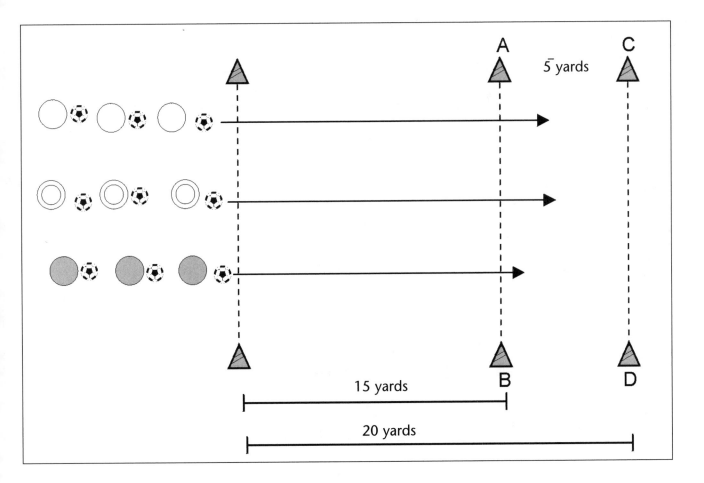

Kick the ball so that it stops behind the line A-B and before the line C-D.
One point is awarded every time a player manages to accurately kick the ball to make it stop between the two lines.
Ten shots for each player.

DRILL 6
Summary table to record and evaluate players' performances

Evaluation / Players	1st Test	2nd Test	3rd Test
	date:	date:	date:
	score	score	score
1			
2			
3			
4			
5			
6			
7			
8			
9			
10			
11			
12			
13			
14			
15			
16			
17			
18			
19			
20			

DRILL 6

Title:
Kicking the ball along the lane

General goal:
Enhancing basic motor skills

Specific goal:
Accurate and powerful shooting

Description:

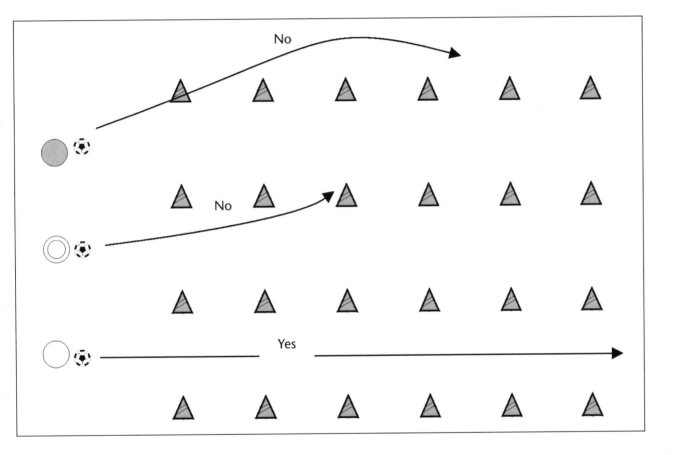

Place some cones in the playing area to mark out some lanes 5 to 10 yards long; the players kick the ball along the lanes so that it does not touch the cones.
One point is awarded to the player who manages to take an accurate shot straight along the lane.
Ten shots for each player.

DRILL 7
Summary table to record and evaluate players' performances

Evaluation Players	1st Test date: no. of wins	2nd Test date: no. of wins	3rd Test date: no. of wins
1			
2			
3			
4			
5			
6			
7			
8			
9			
10			
11			
12			
13			
14			
15			
16			
17			
18			
19			
20			

DRILL 7

Title:
Soccer Bocce

General goal:
Enhancing basic motor skills

Specific goal:
Accurate shooting

Description:

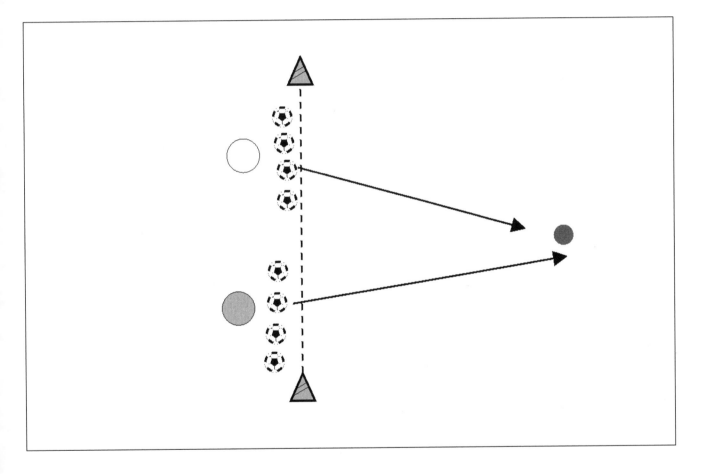

Two players with four balls each; after throwing the small ball (a rubber ball), the two players compete to win a sort of bowling game: they take turns kicking their four balls as near as possible to the small ball.
All the players compete against each other; the player who wins more direct competitions is the winner of the game.

DRILL 8
Summary table to record and evaluate players' performances

Evaluation / Players	1st Test	2nd Test	3rd Test
	date:	date:	date:
	score	score	score
1			
2			
3			
4			
5			
6			
7			
8			
9			
10			
11			
12			
13			
14			
15			
16			
17			
18			
19			
20			

DRILL 8

Title:
Shooting into the hoops

General goal:
Enhancing basic motor skills

Specific goal:
Accurate shooting

Description:

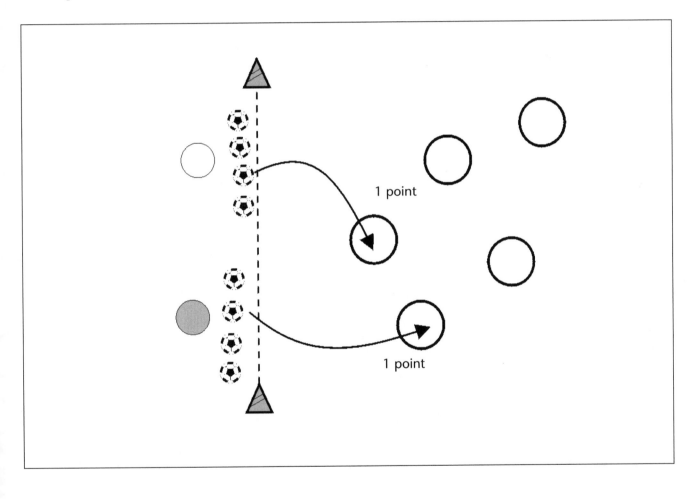

Place some hoops at random on a 15 x 5 yard playing area. The players are standing behind a
"service" line and kick the ball trying to make it stop in the hoops.
One point is awarded every time a player get his ball in one of the hoops.
The player who scores the more points with four balls wins the competition.

DRILL 9
Summary table to record and evaluate players' performances

Evaluation / Players	1st Test date: no. of position	2nd Test date: no. of position	3rd Test date: no. of position
1			
2			
3			
4			
5			
6			
7			
8			
9			
10			
11			
12			
13			
14			
15			
16			
17			
18			
19			
20			

DRILL 9

Title:
Shooting circuit

General goal:
Enhancing basic motor skills

Specific goal:
Accurate and powerful shooting

Description:

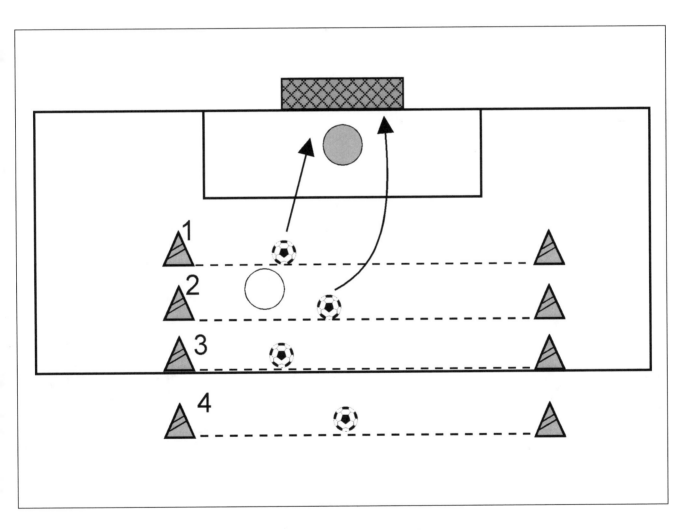

Mark out several lines running parallel with the goal line at different distances from goal. The players shoot at goal from different positions; every time they score a goal, they are allowed to move ahead and shoot from the next line closer to the goal until they reach the winning post.

DRILL 10
Summary table to record and evaluate players' performances

Evaluation / Players	1st Test date:		2nd Test date:		3rd Test date:	
	goals scored with the right foot	goals scored with the left foot	goals scored with the right foot	goals scored with the left foot	goals scored with the right foot	goals scored with the left foot
1						
2						
3						
4						
5						
6						
7						
8						
9						
10						
11						
12						
13						
14						
15						
16						
17						
18						
19						
20						

DRILL 10

Title:
Shooting from different positions

General goal:
Enhancing basic motor skills

Specific goal:
Accurate shooting

Description:

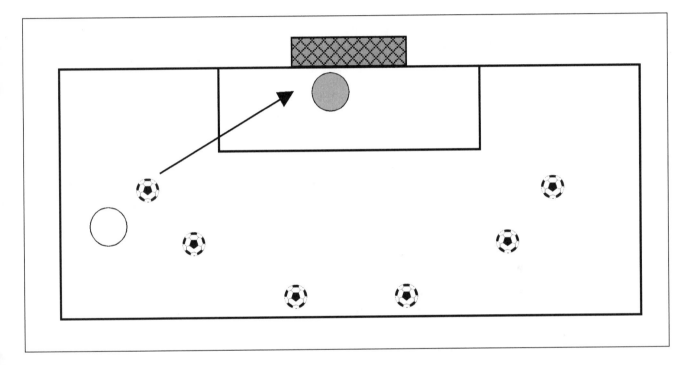

Place six balls in different positions inside the penalty box, at a distance of about 10 yards from the goal. Each player quickly kicks the balls one after the other, trying to score goals.
The player who can score more goals wins the competition.
Alternate one right-footed shot on goal with a left-footed one.

DRILL 11
Summary table to record and evaluate players' performances

Evaluation / Players	1st Test	2nd Test	3rd Test
	date:	date:	date:
	no. of touches	no. of touches	no. of touches
1			
2			
3			
4			
5			
6			
7			
8			
9			
10			
11			
12			
13			
14			
15			
16			
17			
18			
19			
20			

DRILL 11

Title:
Shooting at the small goals

General goal:
Enhancing basic motor skills

Specific goal:
Accurate shooting

Description:

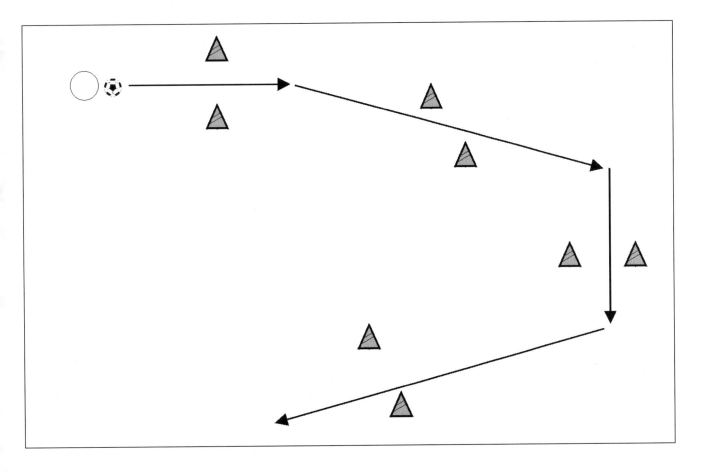

Form a training circuit placing a number of cones on the playing area to mark out several small sized goals. The players dribble and kick the ball through the goals following a specific order.
The player who manages to complete the circuit with the least number of touches of the ball wins the competition.

DRILL 12
Summary table to record and evaluate players' performances

Evaluation / Players	1st Test date: score	2nd Test date: score	3rd Test date: score
1			
2			
3			
4			
5			
6			
7			
8			
9			
10			
11			
12			
13			
14			
15			
16			
17			
18			
19			
20			

DRILL 12

Title:
Shooting in the hexagon

General goal:
Enhancing basic motor skills

Specific goal:
Accurate shooting

Description:

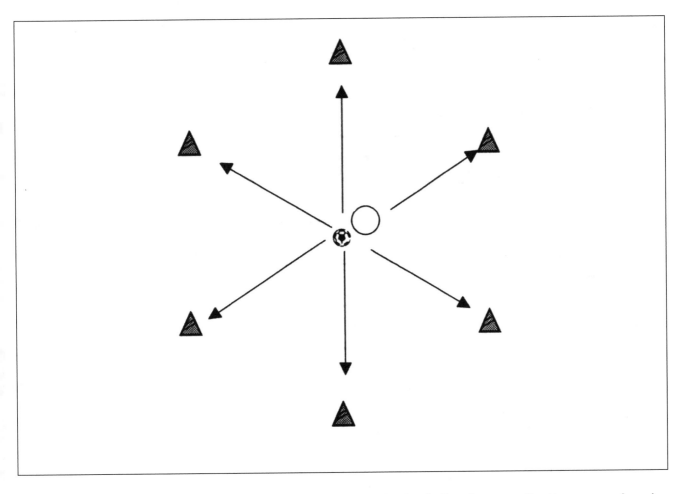

One player is standing in the middle of a hexagon; he kicks the ball trying to strike the cones placed at the six corners of the geometric figure.
The player who strikes all six cones with the smallest number of shots wins the competition.
Each player can take ten shots.

DRILL 13
Summary table to record and evaluate players' performances

Evaluation / Players	1st Test date: score	2nd Test date: score	3rd Test date: score
1			
2			
3			
4			
5			
6			
7			
8			
9			
10			
11			
12			
13			
14			
15			
16			
17			
18			
19			
20			

DRILL 13

Title:
Dribbling through the circuit

General goal:
Enhancing basic motor skills

Specific goal:
Kicking the ball

Description:

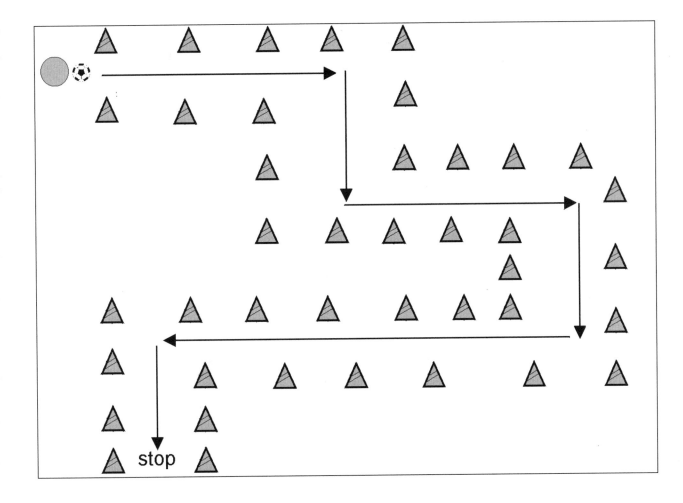

Place a number of cones to form a dribbling circuit in the playing area.
The players kick the ball along the lane trying to avoid making the ball touch the walls
(i.e. the cones).
One point is awarded to those who manage to complete the circuit without the ball touching the cones.
Each player repeats the exercise five times; which player can score more points?

DRILL 14
Summary table to record and evaluate players' performances

Evaluation / Players	1st Test	2nd Test	3rd Test
	date:	date:	date:
	score	score	score
1			
2			
3			
4			
5			
6			
7			
8			
9			
10			
11			
12			
13			
14			
15			
16			
17			
18			
19			
20			

DRILL 14

Title:
Win possession of the ball

General goal:
Enhancing basic motor skills

Specific goal:
Shooting at goal

Description:

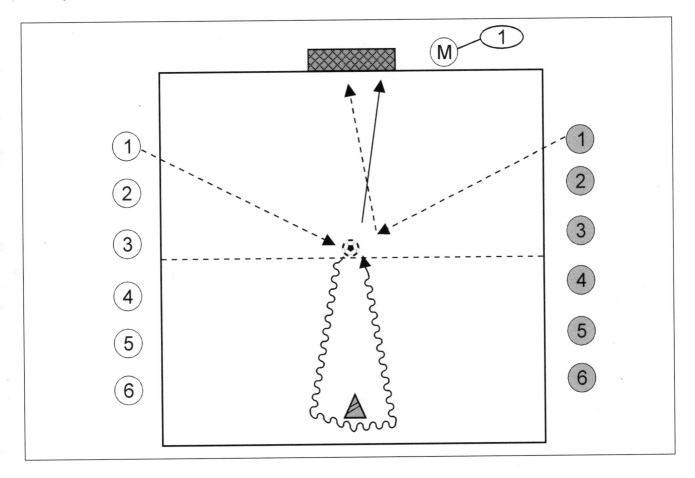

The players are standing behind two opposite lines in front of each other, facing the playing field. When the coach calls a number, the two players who are assigned that number sprint to get possession of the ball in the middle of the playing area. The player who first manages to touch the ball runs backward, dribbles the ball around a cone placed at the edge of the field and then forward to shoot at goal.
The other player with the same number becomes the goalkeeper and quickly sprints to defend the goal. One point is awarded every time a player scores a goal.

DRILL 15
Summary table to record and evaluate players' performances

Evaluation \ Players	1st Test date:		2nd Test date:		3rd Test date:	
	goals scored with the right foot	goals scored with the left foot	goals scored with the right foot	goals scored with the left foot	goals scored with the right foot	goals scored with the left foot
1						
2						
3						
4						
5						
6						
7						
8						
9						
10						
11						
12						
13						
14						
15						
16						
17						
18						
19						
20						

DRILL 15

Title:
Sprint out of the tunnel and shoot

General goal:
Enhancing basic motor skills

Specific goal:
Shooting at goal

Description:

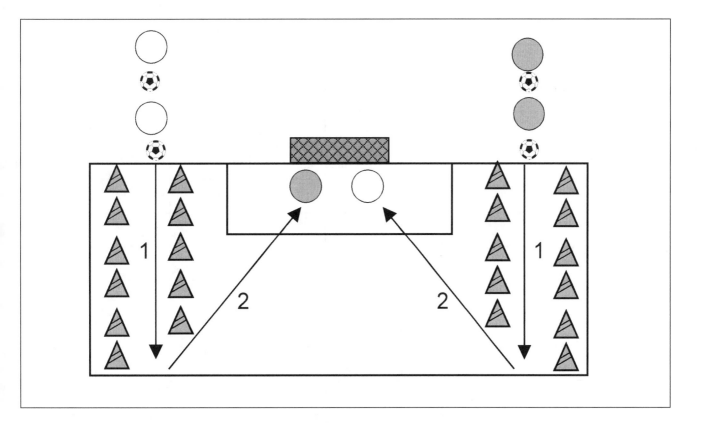

Two lines of players are standing behind the goal line, one on each side of the goal. The first player of each line kicks the ball along a previously marked out lane three yards wide and eight yards long. He runs after the ball, sprints out of the "tunnel" and shoots at goal.
Each player is allowed ten shots on goal: how many goals can he score with the right and the left foot?

DRILL 16
Summary table to record and evaluate players' performances

Evaluation / Players	1st Test date:		2nd Test date:		3rd Test date:	
	points scored with the right foot	points scored with the left foot	points scored with the right foot	points scored with the left foot	points scored with the right foot	points scored with the left foot
1						
2						
3						
4						
5						
6						
7						
8						
9						
10						
11						
12						
13						
14						
15						
16						
17						
18						
19						
20						

DRILL 16

Title:
Free kick

General goal:
Enhancing basic motor skills

Specific goal:
Shooting at goal

Description:

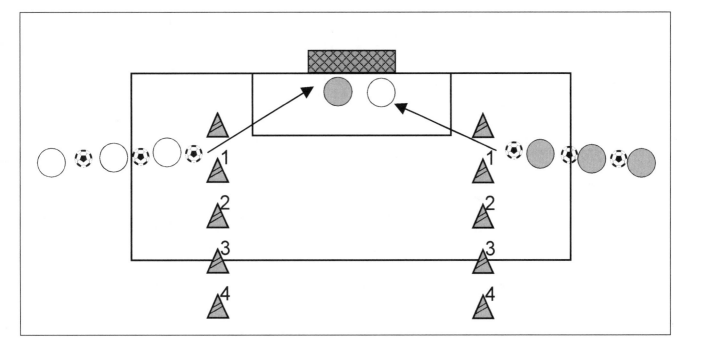

Each player has one ball.
The player places the ball on line No.1 and shoots at goal; if he scores a goal, he moves backward and repeats the exercise from line No.2, otherwise he takes another shot on goal from the same position.
The points are awarded as follows: 1 point if the goal is scored from line No.1; 2 points from line No.2; 3 points from line No.3 and 4 points from line No.4.

DRILL 1
Summary table to record and evaluate players' performances

Evaluation / Players	1st Test	2nd Test	3rd Test
	date:	date:	date:
	time	time	time
1			
2			
3			
4			
5			
6			
7			
8			
9			
10			
11			
12			
13			
14			
15			
16			
17			
18			
19			
20			

DRILL 1

Title:
The labyrinth

General goal:
Enhancing basic motor skills

Specific goal:
Dribbling the ball

Description:

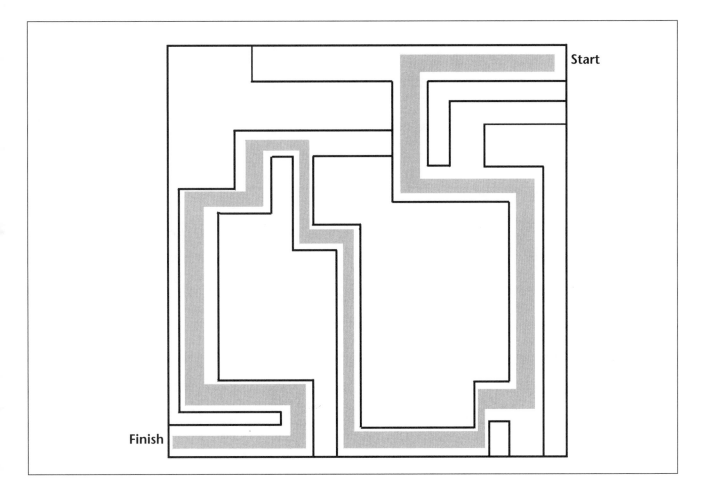

When the coach gives the starting signal, the player sprints and dribbles the ball through the labyrinth, trying to get out of it in the shortest time possible.

DRILL 2
Summary table to record and evaluate players' performances

Evaluation / Players	1st Test	2nd Test	3rd Test
	date:	date:	date:
	time	time	time
1			
2			
3			
4			
5			
6			
7			
8			
9			
10			
11			
12			
13			
14			
15			
16			
17			
18			
19			
20			

DRILL 2

Title:
The four islands

General goal:
Enhancing basic motor skills

Specific goal:
Dribbling the ball

Description:

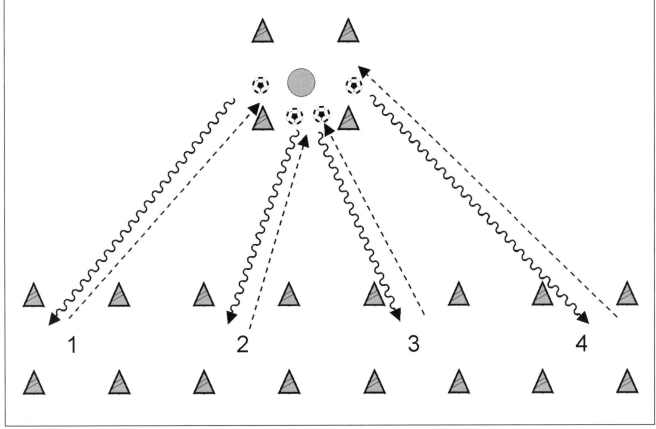

This exercise involves the player dribbling the four balls he has at his disposal to their four respective islands.
How long does it take for him to complete the exercise?

DRILL 3
Summary table to record and evaluate players' performances

Evaluation / Players	1st Test	2nd Test	3rd Test
	date:	date:	date:
	score	score	score
1			
2			
3			
4			
5			
6			
7			
8			
9			
10			
11			
12			
13			
14			
15			
16			
17			
18			
19			
20			

DRILL 3

Title:
Accurate dribble

General goal:
Enhancing basic motor skills

Specific goal:
Dribbling the ball

Description:

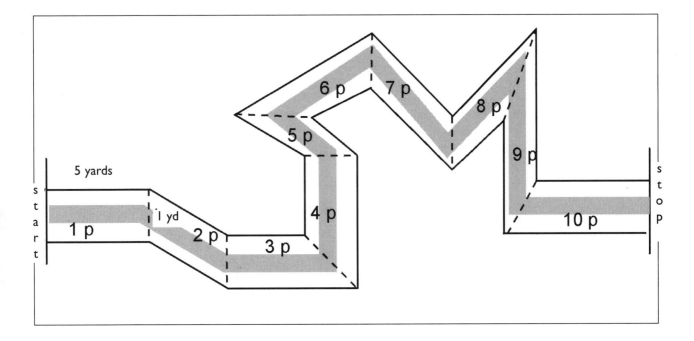

The player has 30 seconds at his disposal to dribble the ball through the labyrinth, avoiding letting the ball roll out of the lines marked out on the field and trying to score as many points as possible. How many points can he score?

DRILL 4
Summary table to record and evaluate players' performances

Evaluation \ Players	1st Test date:	2nd Test date:	3rd Test date:
	score	score	score
1			
2			
3			
4			
5			
6			
7			
8			
9			
10			
11			
12			
13			
14			
15			
16			
17			
18			
19			
20			

DRILL 4

Title:
Dribble the ball home

General goal:
Enhancing basic motor skills

Specific goal:
Dribbling the ball

Description:

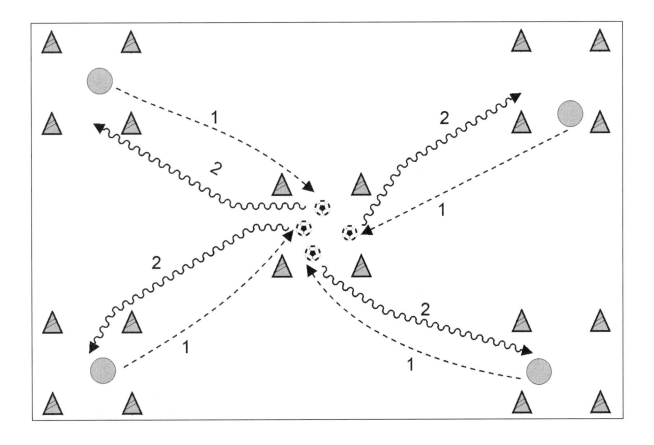

When the coach gives the starting signal, four players start from the four corners of the playing area, they run towards the balls in a square in the middle of the playing area at a distance of about 10 yards from their respective "houses". When they get to the balls, they turn and dribble a ball back to their house and stop the ball inside.
The player who first gets back to his house is awarded 4 points, the second 3 points, the third 2 points and the fourth player 1 point.
Change the groups every time so that all the players compete against each other.

DRILL 5
Summary table to record and evaluate players' performances

Evaluation / Players	1st Test date:		2nd Test date:		3rd Test date:	
	caught by the sparrow hawk	dribbles out of the field	caught by the sparrow hawk	dribbles out of the field	caught by the sparrow hawk	dribbles out of the field
1						
2						
3						
4						
5						
6						
7						
8						
9						
10						
11						
12						
13						
14						
15						
16						
17						
18						
19						
20						

DRILL 5

Title:
The Sparrow Hawk

General goal:
Enhancing basic motor skills

Specific goal:
Dribbling the ball

Description:

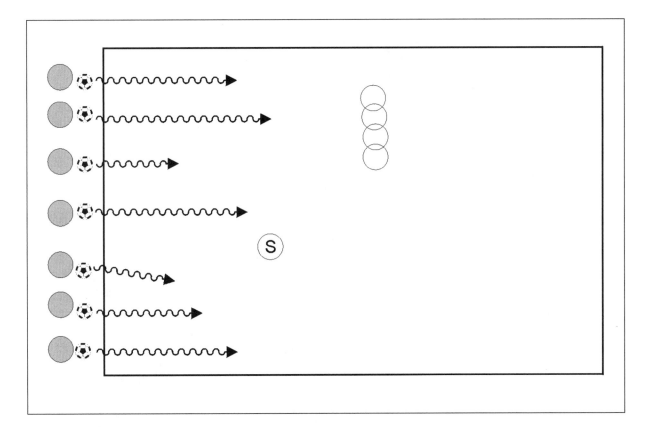

The players are standing at one end of the playing field; when the coach gives the starting signal, they dribble the ball trying to reach the opposite end of the field without being touched by the sparrow hawk (S).
The last player the sparrow hawk touches is the winner of the game.
The players who are touched by the sparrow hawk stand close to each other in a sort of chain to help the sparrow hawk "catch" their teammates.

DRILL 6
Summary table to record and evaluate players' performances

Evaluation / Players	1st Test date: position	2nd Test date: position	3rd Test date: position
1			
2			
3			
4			
5			
6			
7			
8			
9			
10			
11			
12			
13			
14			
15			
16			
17			
18			
19			
20			

DRILL 6

Title:
Dribbling competition

General goal:
Enhancing basic motor skills

Specific goal:
Dribbling the ball

Description:

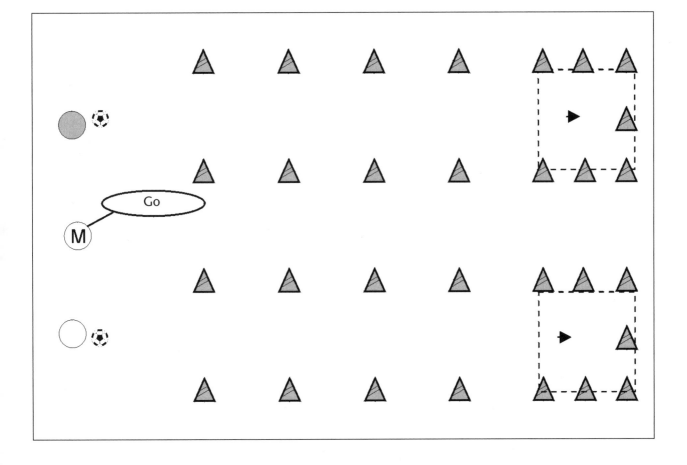

This exercise involves a competition between two players dribbling the ball along two parallel lanes, each one 15 yards long and 2 yards wide.
When the coach gives the starting signal, the two players quickly dribble the ball towards the two respective target areas, while always moving inside the lanes.
The winner directly eliminates the loser from the competition. Who is the winner of the game?

DRILL 7
Summary table to record and evaluate players' performances

Evaluation / Players	1st Test	2nd Test	3rd Test
	date:	date:	date:
	position	position	position
1			
2			
3			
4			
5			
6			
7			
8			
9			
10			
11			
12			
13			
14			
15			
16			
17			
18			
19			
20			

DRILL 7

Title:
Dribbling competition - slalom through the poles

General goal:
Enhancing basic motor skills

Specific goal:
Dribbling the ball

Description:

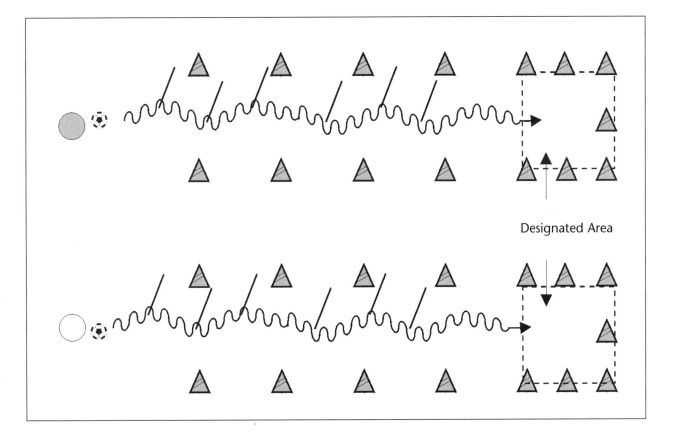

Designated Area

Place a number of cones on the playing area to mark out two lanes 2 yards wide and 18 yards long; place some poles about 3 yards apart inside the lanes.
Two players compete against each other, dribbling the ball towards their respective target areas, making a slalom through the poles.
The winner eliminates the loser (direct elimination).
Who is the winner of the competition?
Draw up the results of the competition.

DRILL 8
Summary table to record and evaluate players' performances

Evaluation / Players	1st Test	2nd Test	3rd Test
	date:	date:	date:
	time	time	time
1			
2			
3			
4			
5			
6			
7			
8			
9			
10			
11			
12			
13			
14			
15			
16			
17			
18			
19			
20			

DRILL 8

Title:
The spiral

General goal:
Enhancing basic motor skills

Specific goal:
Dribbling the ball

Description:

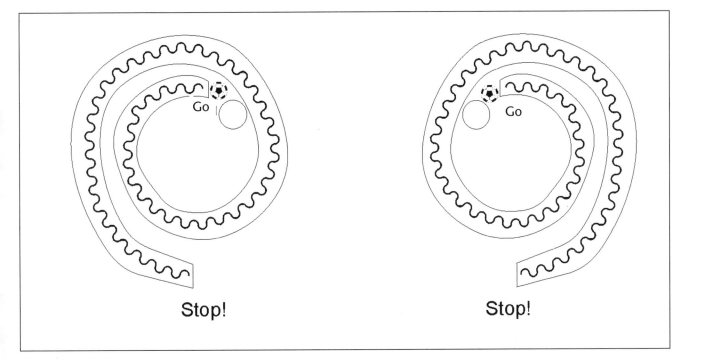

The player first dribbles the ball along a spiral path from the right to the left, and then along a spiral path from the left to the right.
The coach measures and sums up the times that the player takes to dribble the ball through the two circuits, and records them in his summary table.

DRILL 9
Summary table to record and evaluate players' performances

Evaluation / Players	1st Test date:	2nd Test date:	3rd Test date:
	score	score	score
1			
2			
3			
4			
5			
6			
7			
8			
9			
10			
11			
12			
13			
14			
15			
16			
17			
18			
19			
20			

DRILL 9

Title:
Flight through the lane

General goal:
Enhancing basic motor skills

Specific goal:
Dribbling the ball

Description:

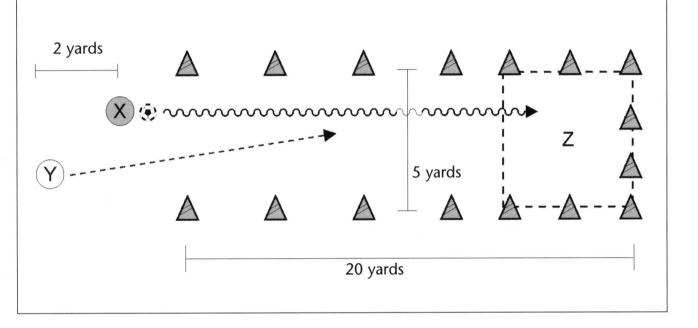

Divide the team in groups of two players each.
The attacking player X dribbles the ball to the target area Z, while also trying to elude the challenging action by the defender Y.
One point is awarded every time a player manages to dribble the ball into the target area.
The defender starts from a position two yards behind the attacking player.

DRILL 10
Summary table to record and evaluate players' performances

Evaluation / Players	1st Test date: score	2nd Test date: score	3rd Test date: score
1			
2			
3			
4			
5			
6			
7			
8			
9			
10			
11			
12			
13			
14			
15			
16			
17			
18			
19			
20			

DRILL 10

Title:
Hunters and Foxes

General goal:
Enhancing basic motor skills

Specific goal:
Dribbling the ball

Description:

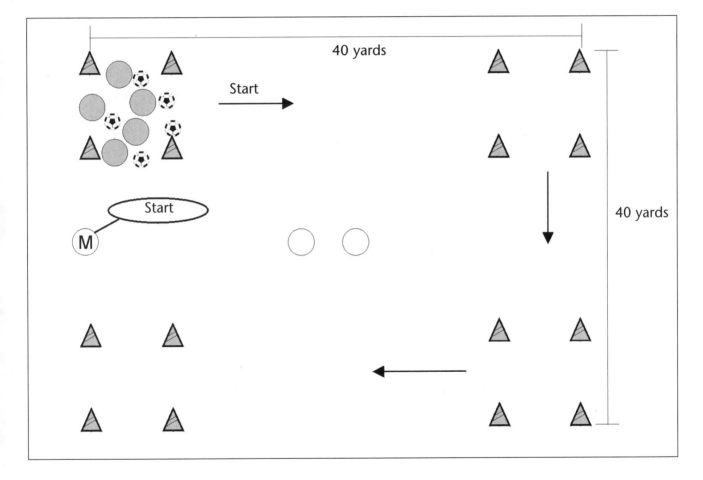

Divide the team in two groups.
When the coach gives the starting signal, the attacking players ⬤ dribble their balls towards the area marked out in front of them, and then towards the next areas.
Two defenders ◯ at a time challenge the attacking players, trying to send their balls out of the playing field.
One point is awarded every time a player manages to dribble the ball into the next area.

DRILL 1
Summary table to record and evaluate players' performances

Evaluation / Players	1st Test date: successful controls	2nd Test date: successful controls	3rd Test date: successful controls
1			
2			
3			
4			
5			
6			
7			
8			
9			
10			
11			
12			
13			
14			
15			
16			
17			
18			
19			
20			

DRILL 1

Title:
Control the ball in the circle

General goal:
Enhancing basic motor skills

Specific goal:
Controlling the ball

Description:

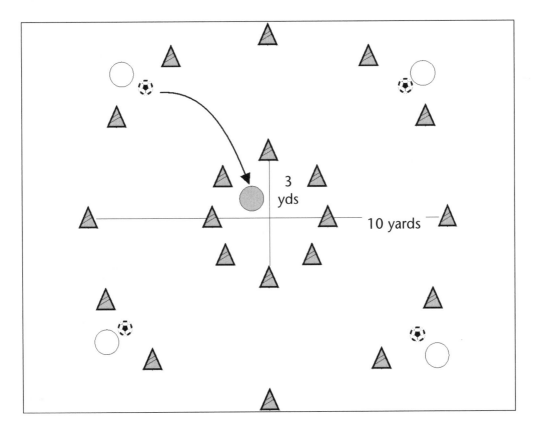

Divide the team in groups of five players each.
Place some cones on the playing field so as to form two concentric circles: one with a diameter of about 10 yards, the other with a diameter of 3 yards.
One player at a time positions inside the small circle while his teammates are standing outside the big one holding a ball in their hands.
In turns, they throw the ball to the player standing inside the small circle, who stops and controls it inside his playing area (successful control).

DRILL 2
Summary table to record and evaluate athletes' performances

Evaluation / Players	1st Test date:			2nd Test date:			3rd Test date:		
	1	3	5	1	3	5	1	3	5
1									
2									
3									
4									
5									
6									
7									
8									
9									
10									
11									
12									
13									
14									
15									
16									
17									
18									
19									
20									

DRILL 2

Title:
Cushion control

General goal:
Enhancing basic motor skills

Specific goal:
Controlling the ball

Description:

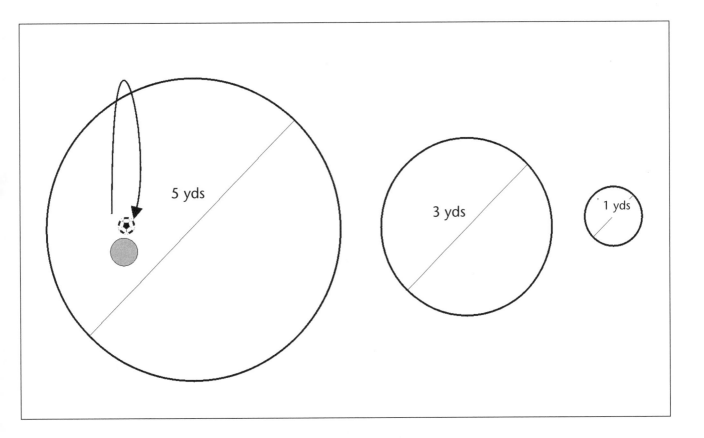

One player at a time throws the ball in the air and tries to control it with the instep inside the various circles (5/3/1 yards of diameter) previously marked out on the playing area.
Every player is allowed three controls in each circle.

DRILL 3
Summary table to record and evaluate athletes' performances

Evaluation / Players	1st Test date:		2nd Test date:		3rd Test date:	
	goals scored with the right foot	goals scored with the left foot	goals scored with the right foot	goals scored with the left foot	goals scored with the right foot	goals scored with the left foot
1						
2						
3						
4						
5						
6						
7						
8						
9						
10						
11						
12						
13						
14						
15						
16						
17						
18						
19						
20						

DRILL 3

Title:
Wedge control

General goal:
Enhancing basic motor skills

Specific goal:
Controlling the ball with the inner instep

Description:

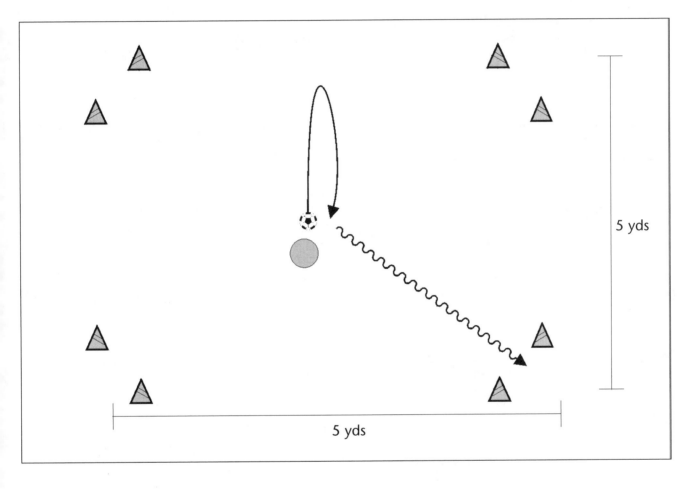

Each player is standing inside a square 5 yards wide holding a ball in his hands. The player throws the ball in the air, lets it bounce on the ground and controls it to shoot:
1) with the right inner instep at the small sized goal on the left and
2) with the left inner instep at the goal on the right.
Five shots on each goal.

DRILL 4
Summary table to record and evaluate athletes' performances

Evaluation / Players	1st Test date:		2nd Test date:		3rd Test date:	
	control on the playing area	control on the playing area	control on the playing area	control on the playing area	control on the playing area	control on the playing area
	right	left	right	left	right	left
1						
2						
3						
4						
5						
6						
7						
8						
9						
10						
11						
12						
13						
14						
15						
16						
17						
18						
19						
20						

DRILL 4

Title:
Control the ball

General goal:
Enhancing basic motor skills

Specific goal:
Controlling the ball while on the run

Description:

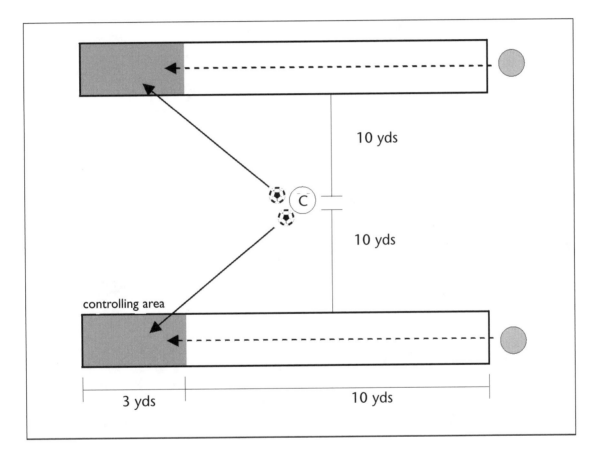

The coach kicks the ball into a special playing area; the player sprints along the marked out lane so as to control and stop the ball in the controlling area at the top of the lane.
Five controls for each player in the right lane and five in the left.

DRILL 5
Summary table to record and evaluate athletes' performances

Evaluation / Players	1st Test	2nd Test	3rd Test
	date:	date:	date:
	score	score	score
1			
2			
3			
4			
5			
6			
7			
8			
9			
10			
11			
12			
13			
14			
15			
16			
17			
18			
19			
20			

DRILL 5

Title:
Control and stop the ball in your own area

General goal:
Enhancing basic motor skills

Specific goal:
Controlling the ball while challenged by an
opponent

Description:

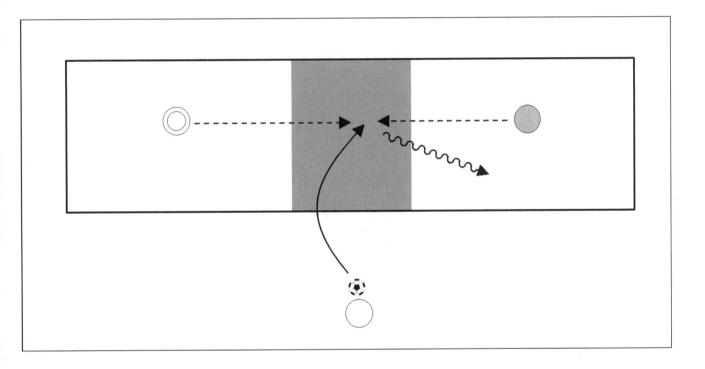

Divide the team in groups of three players each.
In each group two players are standing in the playing area, while the third teammate is standing
outside. The player standing outside throws the ball into the target area and the two players standing
inside run to meet the ball, trying to anticipate their direct opponent. The player who can control and
win possession of the ball dribbles it back and stops it in his own playing area.
One point is awarded to the player who manages to stop the ball in his own playing area.
Ten controls for each pair of players.

DRILL 6
Summary table to record and evaluate athletes' performances

Evaluation / Players	1st Test date: score	2nd Test date: score	3rd Test date: score
1			
2			
3			
4			
5			
6			
7			
8			
9			
10			
11			
12			
13			
14			
15			
16			
17			
18			
19			
20			

DRILL 6

Title:
Control the ball in the cage

General goal:
Enhancing basic motor skills

Specific goal:
Controlling a lob

Description:

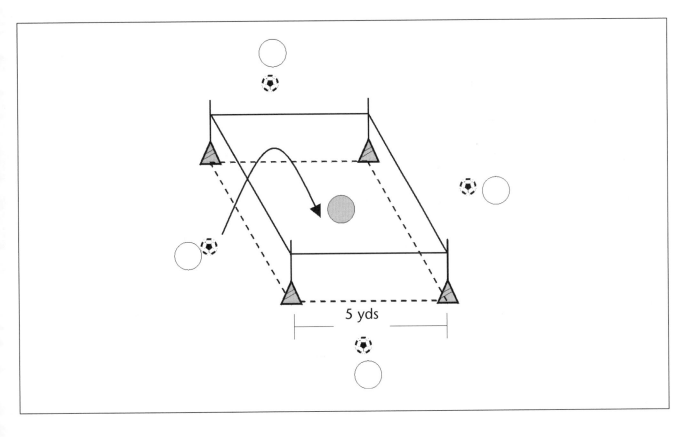

Divide the team in groups of 5 players each.
In turns, one of the 5 players positions inside the cage (a square playing area 5 yards wide marked out by means of four poles and colored tape at a height of about 1.5 yards from the ground).
In turns, one of the four players standing outside the square throws the ball to his teammate standing inside, who controls and stops it.
8 controls for each player; 1 point is awarded every time the player can control the ball successfully.

DRILL 7
Summary table to record and evaluate athletes' performances

Evaluation / Players	1st Test date: score	2nd Test date: score	3rd Test date: score
1			
2			
3			
4			
5			
6			
7			
8			
9			
10			
11			
12			
13			
14			
15			
16			
17			
18			
19			
20			

DRILL 7

Title:
Control and stop the ball

General goal:
Enhancing basic motor skills

Specific goal:
Controlling the ball in restricted spaces

Description:

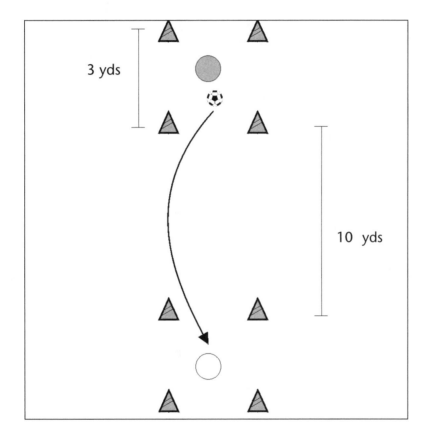

Divide the team in pairs with one ball each.
The two players are standing in front of each other in two opposite squares 3 yards wide and 10 yards apart.
In turns, they pass the ball to each other kicking it with their feet; the player who receives the ball tries to control it with the various parts of his body and stop it inside his own square.
10 controls for each player; one point is awarded every time the player can control the ball successfully.

DRILL 8
Summary table to record and evaluate athletes' performances

Evaluation / Players	1st Test	2nd Test	3rd Test
	date:	date:	date:
	score	score	score
1			
2			
3			
4			
5			
6			
7			
8			
9			
10			
11			
12			
13			
14			
15			
16			
17			
18			
19			
20			

DRILL 8

Title:
Control and stop the ball no.2

General goal:
Enhancing basic motor skills

Specific goal:
Controlling a cross

Description:

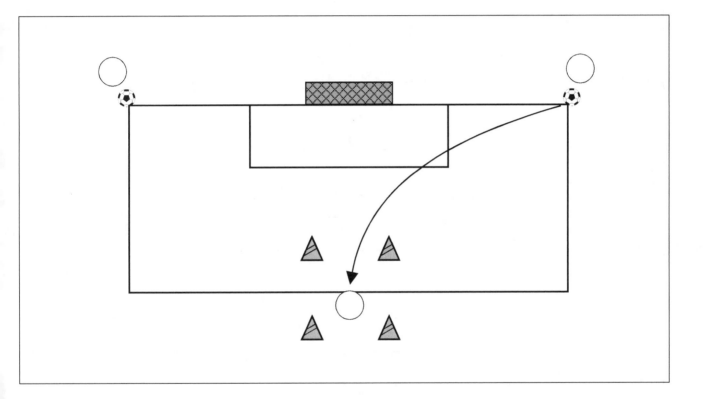

Divide the team in groups of three players each; two balls for each group.
Two players are standing on the goal line at the two corners of the penalty area. In turns, they take a short corner kick towards their third teammate who is standing in a square 3 yards wide at the edge of the penalty box. The player controls and stops the crossed ball inside his playing area.
10 controls for each player; one point is awarded every time the player manages to control the ball inside the square.

DRILL 9
Summary table to record and evaluate athletes' performances

Players \ Evaluation	1st Test date: score	2nd Test date: score	3rd Test date: score
1			
2			
3			
4			
5			
6			
7			
8			
9			
10			
11			
12			
13			
14			
15			
16			
17			
18			
19			
20			

DRILL 9

Title:
Receive and control

General goal:
Enhancing basic motor skills

Specific goal:
Controlling the ball

Description:

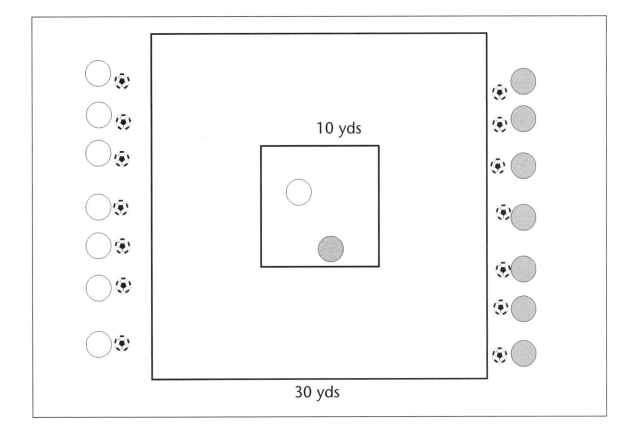

The ● and the ○ are standing at the two opposite sides of a square playing area 30 yards wide facing each other; everybody is holding a ball in his hands. In turns, they throw the ball to their own teammate standing inside the small square. The player who receives the ball controls and stops it within the square, avoiding the challenge by his direct opponent.
Every time a player manages to control the ball successfully he is awarded one point.

DRILL 10
Summary table to record and evaluate athletes' performances

Evaluation / Players	1st Test date: score	2nd Test date: score	3rd Test date: score
1			
2			
3			
4			
5			
6			
7			
8			
9			
10			
11			
12			
13			
14			
15			
16			
17			
18			
19			
20			

DRILL 10

Title:
Control in the target area

General goal:
Enhancing basic motor skills

Specific goal:
Controlling the ball

Description:

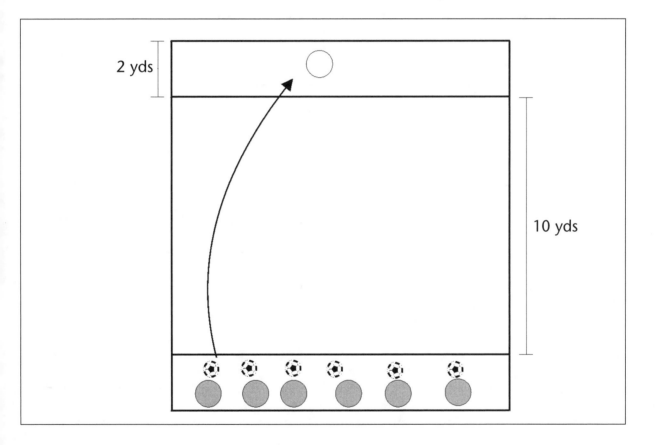

Players ⬤ are holding one ball each in their hands; in turns, they take a throw-in so as to throw the ball into the opposite two yard wide target area.
Player ◯ controls and stops the ball inside that area.
He is awarded one point if he does not let the ball roll outside.
Five controls for each player.

DRILL 1
Summary table to record and evaluate athletes' performances

Evaluation / Players	1st Test	2nd Test	3rd Test
	date:	date:	date:
	results	results	results
1			
2			
3			
4			
5			
6			
7			
8			
9			
10			
11			
12			
13			
14			
15			
16			
17			
18			
19			
20			

DRILL 1

Title:
Heading at goal

General goal:
Enhancing basic motor skills

Specific goal:
Heading skills

Description:

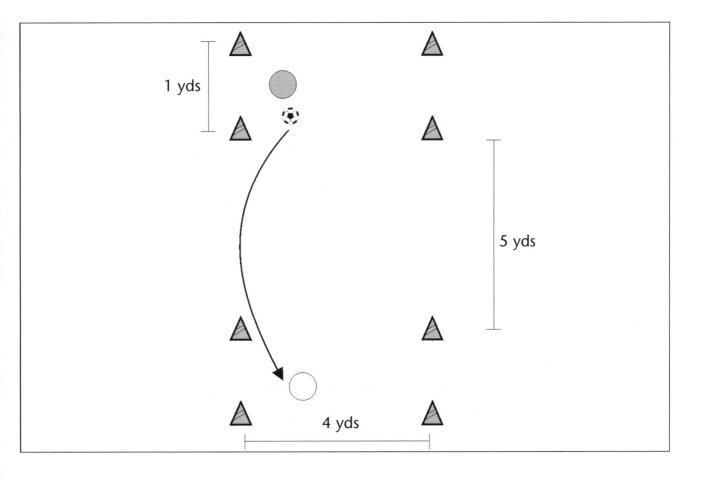

Divide the team in several groups of two players each.
In turns, one of the two players kicks the ball to himself in the air and heads it trying to score a goal to his teammate who is standing in front of him.
The player can move within a 1 by 4 yard area for his run up.
Every player is allowed five headers in each game.
Knock-out competition.

DRILL 2
Summary table to record and evaluate athletes' performances

Evaluation / Players	1st Test	2nd Test	3rd Test
	date:	date:	date:
	score	score	score
1			
2			
3			
4			
5			
6			
7			
8			
9			
10			
11			
12			
13			
14			
15			
16			
17			
18			
19			
20			

DRILL 2

Title:
Center the hoop

General goal:
Enhancing basic motor skills

Specific goal:
Heading skills

Description:

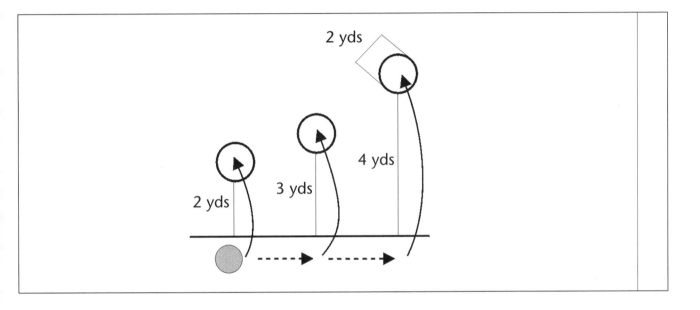

One ball for each player.
The player tosses the ball up to himself and heads it so as to make it bounce into the hoop lying in front of him.
The three hoops are placed down on the ground at different distances from the player; three headers into each hoop.
One point is awarded every time the player can center the hoop.

DRILL 3
Summary table to record and evaluate athletes' performances

Evaluation / Players	1st Test date: no. of heading juggles	2nd Test date: no. of heading juggles	3rd Test date: no. of heading juggles
1			
2			
3			
4			
5			
6			
7			
8			
9			
10			
11			
12			
13			
14			
15			
16			
17			
18			
19			
20			

DRILL 3

Title:
Heading juggles against a wall

General goal:
Enhancing basic motor skills

Specific goal:
Heading skills

Description:

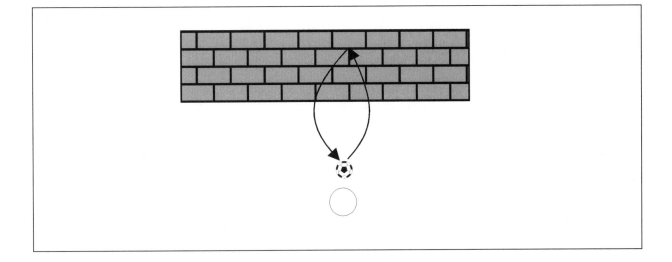

One ball for each player who repeatedly heads the ball against a wall without letting it fall to the ground.
How many heading juggles without the ball bouncing on the ground?
Every player can repeat the exercise three times; choose the best performance.

DRILL 4
Summary table to record and evaluate athletes' performances

Evaluation / Players	1st Test date: distance	2nd Test date: distance	3rd Test date: distance
1			
2			
3			
4			
5			
6			
7			
8			
9			
10			
11			
12			
13			
14			
15			
16			
17			
18			
19			
20			

DRILL 4

Title:
Long header

General goal:
Enhancing basic motor skills

Specific goal:
Heading skills

Description:

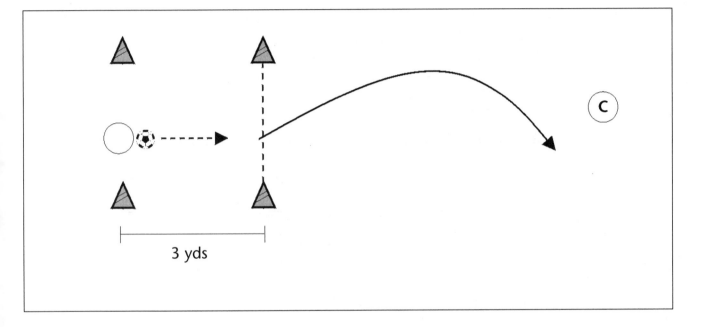

One ball for each player.
The player takes a run up of 3 yards at most, throws the ball to himself in the air and heads it trying to make it bounce as far as possible.
The coach measures the distance using a tape measure.
Three headers for each player.

DRILL 5
Summary table to record and evaluate athletes' performances

Evaluation / Players	1st Test	2nd Test	3rd Test
	date:	date:	date:
	score	score	score
1			
2			
3			
4			
5			
6			
7			
8			
9			
10			
11			
12			
13			
14			
15			
16			
17			
18			
19			
20			

DRILL 5

Title:
Heading at the upper corner of the net

General goal:
Enhancing basic motor skills

Specific goal:
Heading skills

Description:

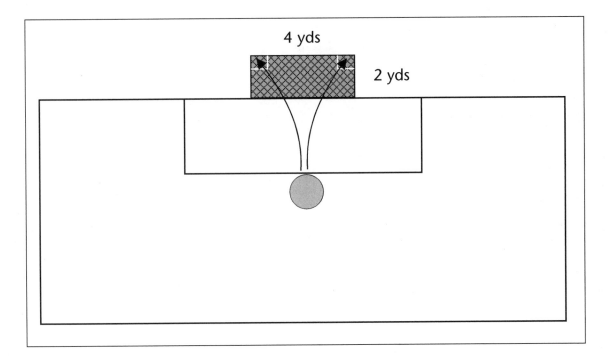

One ball for each player. One player at a time is standing in a central position at the edge of the goal area and heads the ball trying to direct it at the upper corner of the net.
Five headers for each player.
One point is awarded for each goal the player scores.

DRILL 6
Summary table to record and evaluate athletes' performances

Evaluation / Players	1st Test date: no. of heading juggles	2nd Test date: no. of heading juggles	3rd Test date: no. of heading juggles
1			
2			
3			
4			
5			
6			
7			
8			
9			
10			
11			
12			
13			
14			
15			
16			
17			
18			
19			
20			

DRILL 6

Title:
Heading competition

General goal:
Enhancing basic motor skills

Specific goal:
Heading skills

Description:

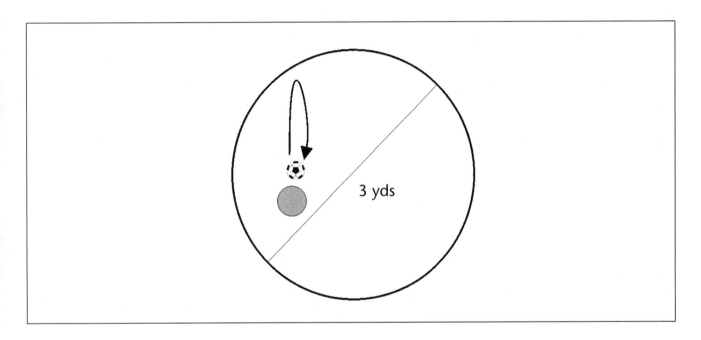

One player at a time heads the ball repeatedly without letting it fall to the ground while moving circle of 3 yard circle.
Every player can repeat the exercise three times. Count the number of heading juggles the player can make consecutively without moving out of the circle.

DRILL 7
Summary table to record and evaluate athletes' performances

Evaluation / Players	1st Test	2nd Test	3rd Test
	date:	date:	date:
	score	score	score
1			
2			
3			
4			
5			
6			
7			
8			
9			
10			
11			
12			
13			
14			
15			
16			
17			
18			
19			
20			

DRILL 7

Title:
Heading the ball while walking

General goal:
Enhancing basic motor skills

Specific goal:
Heading skills

Description:

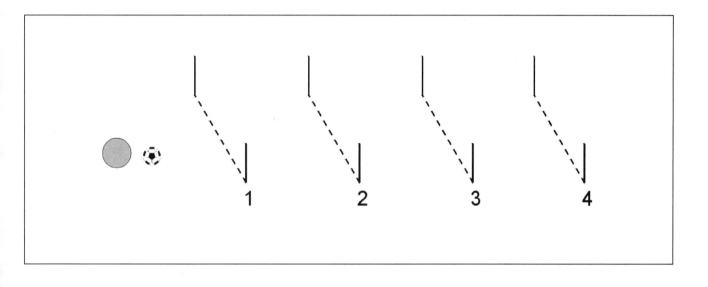

The player in possession of the ball moves while heading the ball repeatedly at the same time.
He tries to walk along a straight track previously marked by means of special poles placed two yards apart.
The player is awarded one point every time he can cross a new target line.
Record the best score out of five performances for each player.

DRILL 8
Summary table to record and evaluate athletes' performances

Evaluation / Players	1st Test date: score	2nd Test date: score	3rd Test date: score
1			
2			
3			
4			
5			
6			
7			
8			
9			
10			
11			
12			
13			
14			
15			
16			
17			
18			
19			
20			

DRILL 8

Title:
Bowling competition

General goal:
Enhancing basic motor skills

Specific goal:
Heading skills

Description:

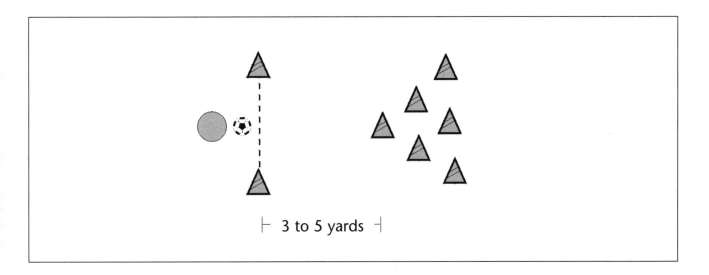

├ 3 to 5 yards ┤

The player in possession of the ball tosses it up to himself and heads it, trying to strike as many cones as possible. The cones are placed at a distance that can range from 3 to 5 yards from the player.
The player is awarded one point for each cone he knocks down.
Five headers for each player.

SECOND LEVEL DRILLS

This chapter includes drills belonging to the second level. These were carefully selected and can be used to achieve the second goal of this coaching educational method, while also reinforcing and enhancing all those skills and movements previously dealt with in the first phase of this coaching progression.

All the exercises I am going to suggest in the following pages can be performed either individually or in small groups and practically aim at "combining acquired basic movements and coaching individual tactical skills".

Two different pages providing the reader with special directions are dedicated to each drill: the first page shows a helpful summary table that can help the coach record and evaluate athletes' results so as to constantly monitor their performances; the second page includes the title of the drill, both the general and specific goals that the coach tries to pursue with that particular exercise and the description of the drill combined with the field diagram.

The following drills are based on a few simple rules that can be easily understood. In this case too, individual practice still prevails over team work in order to achieve the final goal of the game.

If the coach has properly explained and coached basic motor skills, such technical movements as kicking, dribbling or controlling the ball have now become more automatic and well coordinated. This is why the need to combine all the various skills and movements the player has gradually acquired naturally emerges in this phase.

In this chapter focusing on second level drills, we are going to suggest special activities that aim at helping young players gradually understand that any movement and skill in soccer is not an end in itself but has a real and practical purpose, since it is always applied to real game situations.

Basic acquired skills will be combined as follows:
- juggling + shooting skills
- heading + shooting skills
- dribbling + shooting skills
- controlling + dribbling skills
- controlling + shooting skills
- controlling + dribbling + shooting skills

DRILL 1
Summary table to record and evaluate athletes' performances

Evaluation ⟍ Players	1st Test	2nd Test	3rd Test
	date:	date:	date:
	score	score	score
1			
2			
3			
4			
5			
6			
7			
8			
9			
10			
11			
12			
13			
14			
15			
16			
17			
18			
19			
20			

DRILL 1

Title:
Juggle and shoot

General goal:
Combining basic technical skills

Specific goal:
Enhancing juggling and shooting skills

Description:

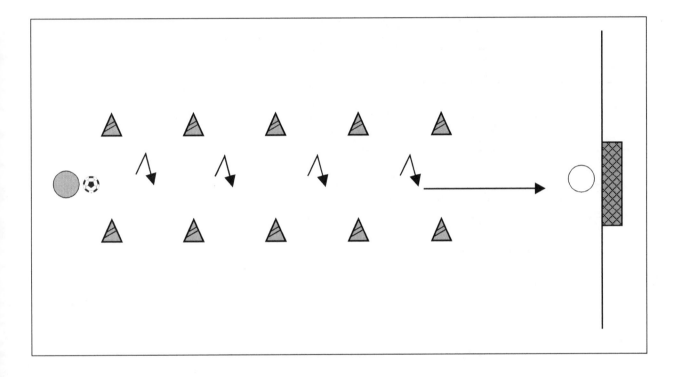

Every player is holding a ball in his hands.
When the coach gives the starting signal, the player juggles the ball once in each square and takes the ball in his hands again. When he arrives in the last square, he juggles the ball and shoots at goal trying to score.
How many goals can he score out of ten shots on goal?
One point is awarded for each goal.

DRILL 2
Summary table to record and evaluate athletes' performances

Evaluation / Players	1st Test date: score	2nd Test date: score	3rd Test date: score
1			
2			
3			
4			
5			
6			
7			
8			
9			
10			
11			
12			
13			
14			
15			
16			
17			
18			
19			
20			

DRILL 2

Title:
Juggling and shooting competition

General goal:
Combining basic technical skills

Specific goal:
Enhancing juggling and shooting skills

Description:

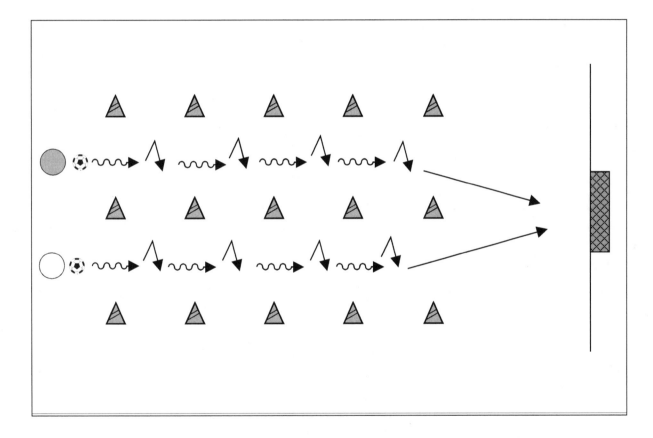

The two players in possession of the ball juggle it once in each square until they reach the position from where they can shoot at goal.
One point is awarded to the player who scores first.
The game involves no goalkeepers.

DRILL 3
Summary table to record and evaluate athletes' performances

Evaluation / Players	1st Test date: / score	2nd Test date: / score	3rd Test date: / score
1			
2			
3			
4			
5			
6			
7			
8			
9			
10			
11			
12			
13			
14			
15			
16			
17			
18			
19			
20			

DRILL 3

Title:
Juggling and shooting competition - slalom
through the poles

General goal:
Combining basic technical skills

Specific goal:
Enhancing juggling and shooting skills

Description:

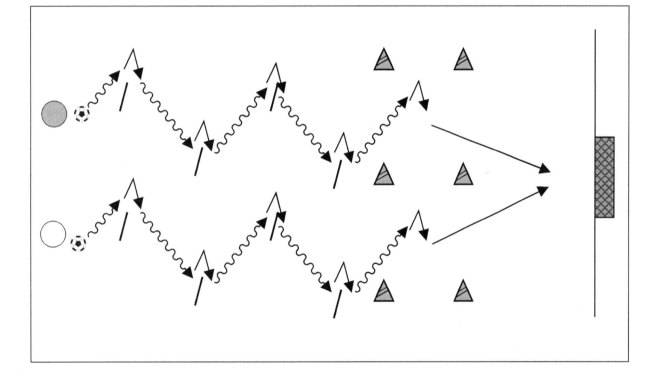

Divide the team in two or more subgroups.
One ball for each player.
When the coach gives the starting signal, the two players juggle the ball once at each pole until they
get to the shooting area and take a shot on goal.
One point is awarded to the player who scores first.
The game involves no goalkeepers.
How many points can the player score out of ten shots on goal?

DRILL 4
Summary table to record and evaluate athletes' performances

Evaluation \ Players	1st Test	2nd Test	3rd Test
	date:	date:	date:
	score	score	score
1			
2			
3			
4			
5			
6			
7			
8			
9			
10			
11			
12			
13			
14			
15			
16			
17			
18			
19			
20			

DRILL 4

Title:
Juggling and shooting competition on the spot

General goal:
Combining basic technical skills

Specific goal:
Enhancing juggling and shooting skills

Description:

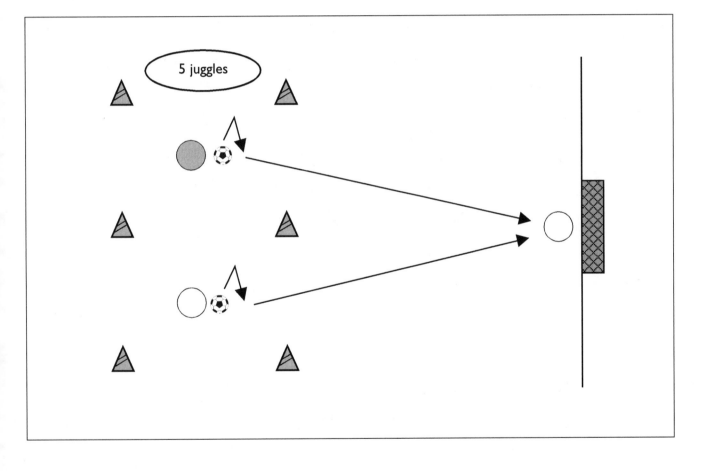

Divide the team in two or more subgroups; one ball for each player.
In turns, two players at a time are standing inside two squares; they juggle the ball five times and shoot at goal.
One point is awarded to the player who scores first.
Ten shots on goal for each player: how many goals?

DRILL 5
Summary table to record and evaluate athletes' performances

Evaluation / Players	1st Test	2nd Test	3rd Test
	date:	date:	date:
	score	score	score
1			
2			
3			
4			
5			
6			
7			
8			
9			
10			
11			
12			
13			
14			
15			
16			
17			
18			
19			
20			

DRILL 5

Title:
Juggle and hook volley shot on goal

General goal:
Combining basic technical skills

Specific goal:
Enhancing juggling and shooting skills

Description:

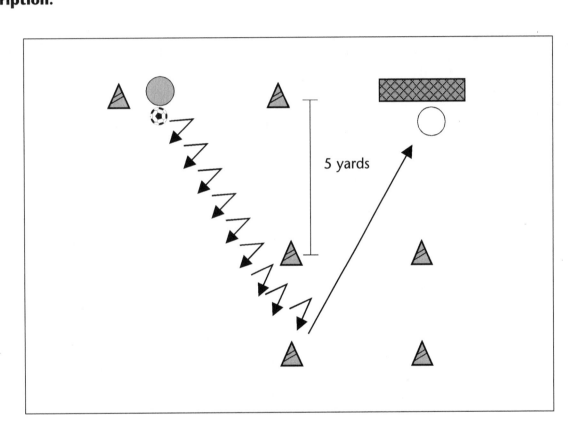

The player in possession juggles the ball towards the shooting area and takes a hook volley shot on goal.
One point is awarded when the player completes the exercise but no goal is scored; two points if the player scores a goal.
Ten shots on goal for each player.

DRILL 1
Summary table to record and evaluate athletes' performances

Evaluation / Players	1st Test date:		2nd Test date:		3rd Test date:	
	score right foot	score left foot	score right foot	score left foot	score right foot	score left foot
1						
2						
3						
4						
5						
6						
7						
8						
9						
10						
11						
12						
13						
14						
15						
16						
17						
18						
19						
20						

DRILL 1

Title:
Dribble and shot on goal

General goal:
Combining basic motor skills

Specific goal:
Enhancing dribbling and shooting skills

Description:

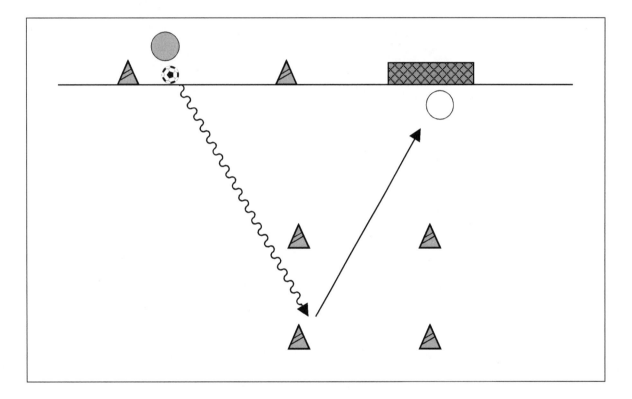

Starting from the cone placed on the goal line, player I dribbles the ball up to the square previously marked out on the playing field; when he arrives in the square, he shoots at goal trying to score.
5 shots with the right foot and 5 shots with the left one.
Every time the player scores a goal he is awarded one point.

DRILL 2
Summary table to record and evaluate athletes' performances

Evaluation / Players	1st Test date:		2nd Test date:		3rd Test date:	
	score right foot	score left foot	score right foot	score left foot	score right foot	score left foot
1						
2						
3						
4						
5						
6						
7						
8						
9						
10						
11						
12						
13						
14						
15						
16						
17						
18						
19						
20						

DRILL 2

Title:
Dribble along the track and shot on goal

General goal:
Combining basic motor skills

Specific goal:
Enhancing dribbling and shooting skills

Description:

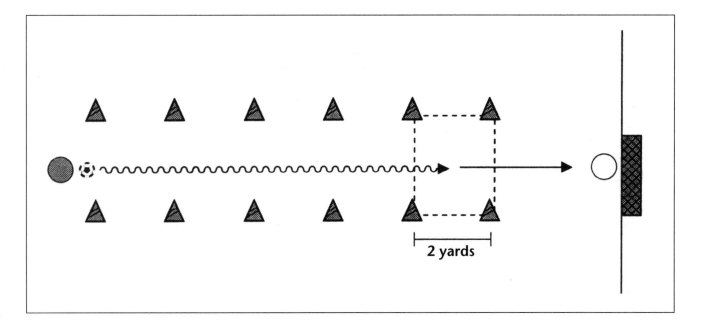

Player ⬤ is in possession of the ball. He dribbles the ball along a straight track towards the shooting area; when he enters this area he can shoot at goal and try to score.
5 shots on goal with the right foot and 5 shots with the left.
One point is awarded for each goal.
The player becomes the goalkeeper immediately after taking a shot on goal.

DRILL 3
Summary table to record and evaluate athletes' performances

Evaluation / Players	1st Test date:		2nd Test date:		3rd Test date:	
	score right foot	score left foot	score right foot	score left foot	score right foot	score left foot
1						
2						
3						
4						
5						
6						
7						
8						
9						
10						
11						
12						
13						
14						
15						
16						
17						
18						
19						
20						

DRILL 3

Title:
Dribble and shot on goal from a side position

General goal:
Combining basic motor skills

Specific goal:
Enhancing dribbling and shooting skills

Description:

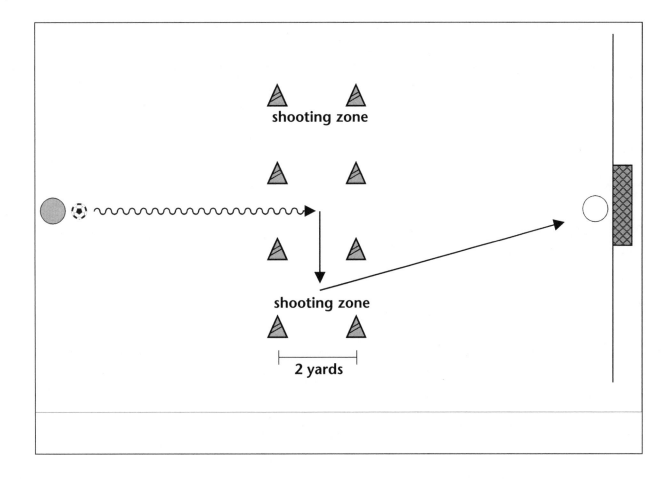

Player ● dribbles the ball up into the central square marked out in front of him and then kicks it either into the right shooting area or into the left one to shoot at goal.
5 shots on goal with the right foot and 5 with the left.
One point is awarded for each goal.

DRILL 4
Summary table to record and evaluate athletes' performances

Evaluation / Players	1st Test date:		2nd Test date:		3rd Test date:	
	score right foot	score left foot	score right foot	score left foot	score right foot	score left foot
1						
2						
3						
4						
5						
6						
7						
8						
9						
10						
11						
12						
13						
14						
15						
16						
17						
18						
19						
20						

DRILL 4

Title:
Slalom through the cones and shot on goal

General goal:
Combining basic motor skills

Specific goal:
Enhancing dribbling and shooting skills

Description:

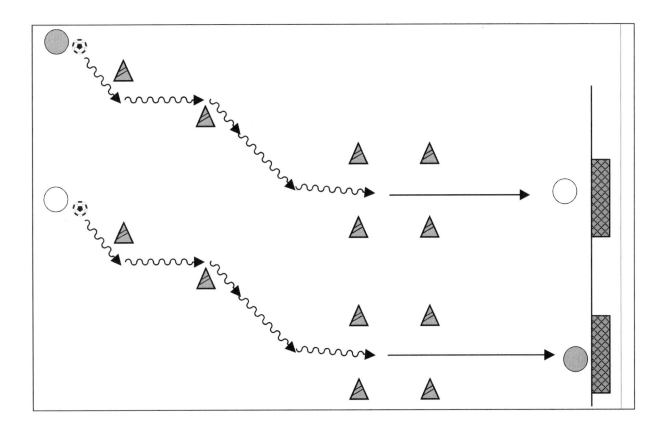

When the coach gives the starting signal players
⬤ and ◯ dribble the ball through the cones.
When they reach their respective shooting areas, they can shoot at goal.
One point for each goal.
The player who scores first is awarded two points.
5 shots on goal with the right foot and 5 with the left.

DRILL 5
Summary table to record and evaluate athletes' performances

Evaluation / Players	1st Test date:		2nd Test date:		3rd Test date:	
	score right foot	score left foot	score right foot	score left foot	score right foot	score left foot
1						
2						
3						
4						
5						
6						
7						
8						
9						
10						
11						
12						
13						
14						
15						
16						
17						
18						
19						
20						

DRILL 5

Title:
Dribbling and shooting competition

General goal:
Combining basic motor skills

Specific goal:
Enhancing dribbling and shooting skills

Description:

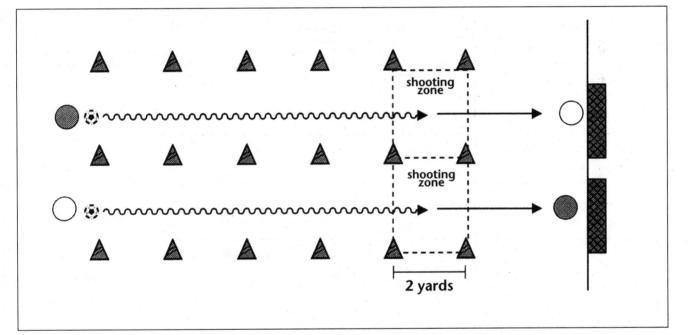

When the coach gives the starting signal, players
● and ○ dribble the ball ahead towards their respective shooting areas and shoot at goal.
The player who can score a goal first is awarded two points, the other one point.
The players are allowed to shoot with their favorite foot.
5 shots on goal, each with a different opponent.

DRILL 1
Summary table to record and evaluate athletes' performances

Evaluation ⟋ Players	1st Test	2nd Test	3rd Test
	date:	date:	date:
	no. of goals	no. of goals	no. of goals
1			
2			
3			
4			
5			
6			
7			
8			
9			
10			
11			
12			
13			
14			
15			
16			
17			
18			
19			
20			

DRILL 1

Title:
Head and shoot

General goal:
Combining basic motor skills

Specific goal:
Enhancing heading and shooting skills

Description:

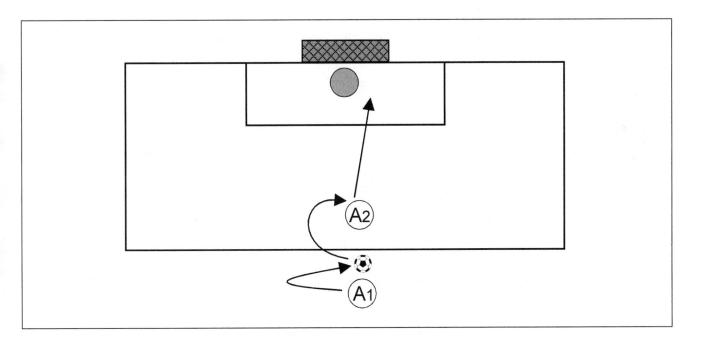

The player in possession of the ball starts from the edge of the penalty area, throws the ball in the air, heads it, lets it bounce once on the ground and shoots at goal.
Ten shots for each player: how many goals?

DRILL 2
Summary table to record and evaluate athletes' performances

Evaluation / Players	1st Test	2nd Test	3rd Test
	date:	date:	date:
	score	score	score
1			
2			
3			
4			
5			
6			
7			
8			
9			
10			
11			
12			
13			
14			
15			
16			
17			
18			
19			
20			

DRILL 2

Title:
Head the ball into the square and shoot at goal

General goal:
Combining basic motor skills

Specific goal:
Enhancing heading and shooting skills

Description:

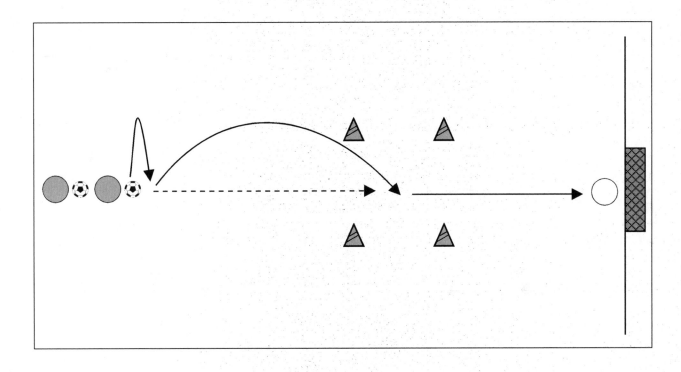

One ball for each player.
The player throws the ball to himself in the air and heads it trying to direct it into the shooting area in front of him (a square 5 yards wide). From this position, he takes a shot on goal.
One point is awarded for each goal scored.

DRILL 3
Summary table to record and evaluate athletes' performances

Evaluation / Players	1st Test	2nd Test	3rd Test
	date:	date:	date:
	score	score	score
1			
2			
3			
4			
5			
6			
7			
8			
9			
10			
11			
12			
13			
14			
15			
16			
17			
18			
19			
20			

DRILL 3

Title:
Heading juggle and shot on goal

General goal:
Combining basic motor skills

Specific goal:
Enhancing heading and shooting skills

Description:

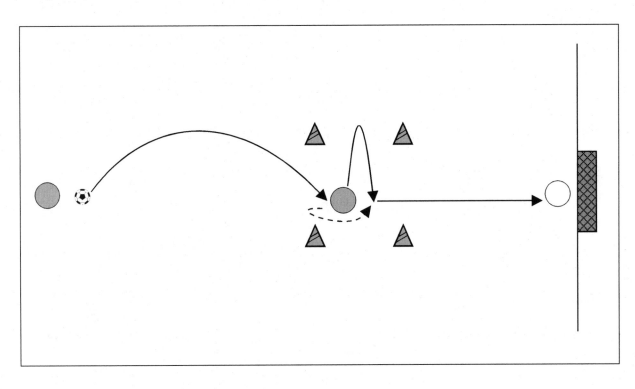

One ball for each pair of players. Player A throws the ball to his teammate B, who heads the ball,
lets it bounce on the ground once, turns round so as to face the goal and shoots at goal.
The pair are awarded one point for each goal they score.

DRILL 4
Summary table to record and evaluate athletes' performances

Evaluation / Players	1st Test	2nd Test	3rd Test
	date:	date:	date:
	score	score	score
1			
2			
3			
4			
5			
6			
7			
8			
9			
10			
11			
12			
13			
14			
15			
16			
17			
18			
19			
20			

DRILL 4

Title:
3 headers and final shot on goal

General goal:
Combining basic motor skills

Specific goal:
Enhancing heading and shooting skills

Description:

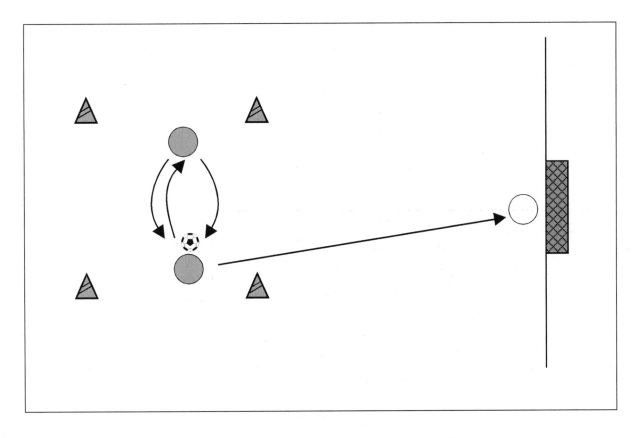

One ball for each pair of players.
The two players head the ball to each other three times, at least, while always standing within a square playing area 5 yards wide; after three headers or more one of the two teammates can shoot at goal.
The pair are awarded one point for each goal they score.

DRILL 5
Summary table to record and evaluate athletes' performances

Evaluation / Players	1st Test	2nd Test	3rd Test
	date:	date:	date:
	score	score	score
1			
2			
3			
4			
5			
6			
7			
8			
9			
10			
11			
12			
13			
14			
15			
16			
17			
18			
19			
20			

DRILL 5

Title:
Heading pass and shot on goal

General goal:
Combining basic motor skills

Specific goal:
Enhancing heading and shooting skills

Description:

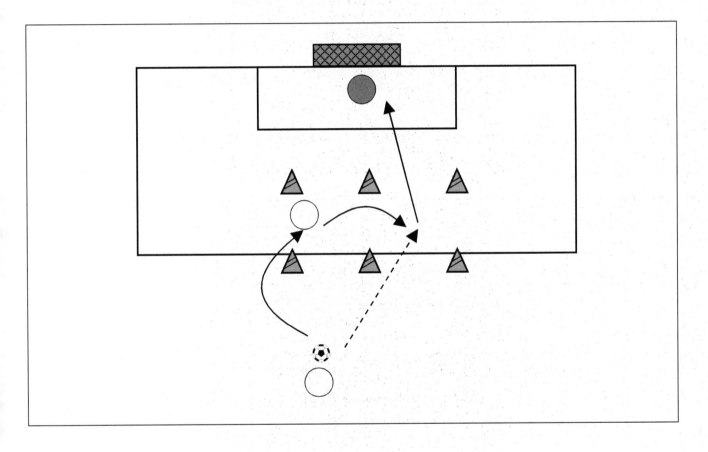

One ball for each pair of players.
Player A throws the ball to his teammate B who passes it back to A heading the ball sideways into the near shooting square area; player A sprints into the shooting area and takes a shot on goal.
The pair are awarded one point for each goal they score.

DRILL 1
Summary table to record and evaluate athletes' performances

Evaluation / Players	1st Test	2nd Test	3rd Test
	date:	date:	date:
	score	score	score
1			
2			
3			
4			
5			
6			
7			
8			
9			
10			
11			
12			
13			
14			
15			
16			
17			
18			
19			
20			

DRILL 1

Title:
Pass by the goalkeeper, control and shot on goal

General goal:
Combining basic motor skills

Specific goal:
Enhancing controlling and shooting skills

Description:

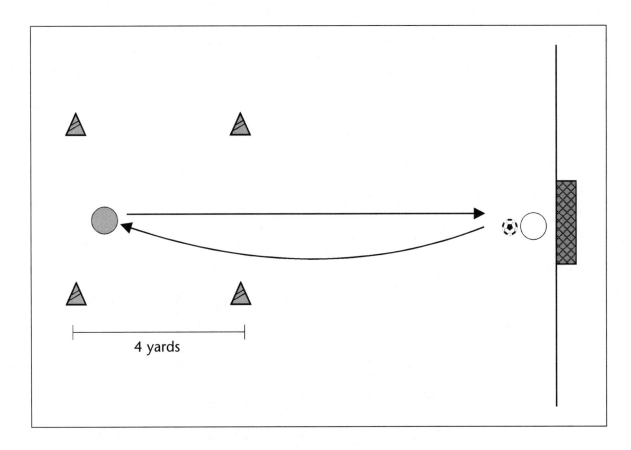

4 yards

The goalkeeper throws the ball to the player standing in front of him at a distance of about 10 yards; the player receives the ball, controls it in his square playing area 4 yards wide and takes a shot on goal.
Ten shots for each player; one point for each goal scored.

DRILL 2
Summary table to record and evaluate athletes' performances

Evaluation / Players	1st Test date: score	2nd Test date: score	3rd Test date: score
1			
2			
3			
4			
5			
6			
7			
8			
9			
10			
11			
12			
13			
14			
15			
16			
17			
18			
19			
20			

DRILL 2

Title:
Direct the ball and shoot at goal

General goal:
Combining basic motor skills

Specific goal:
Enhancing controlling and shooting skills

Description:

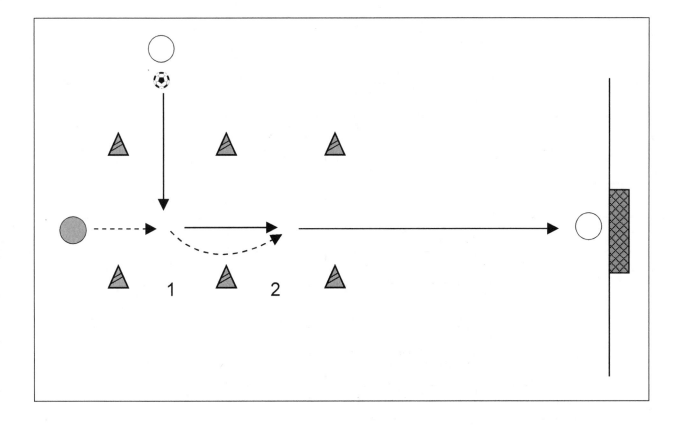

Player A passes the ball to his teammate B, who controls the ball in the square no. 1 and directs it ahead in the square no. 2, where he can shoot at goal.
He is awarded one point if he scores a goal.

DRILL 3
Summary table to record and evaluate athletes' performances

Evaluation / Players	1st Test	2nd Test	3rd Test
	date:	date:	date:
	results	results	results
1			
2			
3			
4			
5			
6			
7			
8			
9			
10			
11			
12			
13			
14			
15			
16			
17			
18			
19			
20			

DRILL 3

Title:
Control and dribble

General goal:
Combining basic motor skills

Specific goal:
Enhancing controlling and dribbling skills

Description:

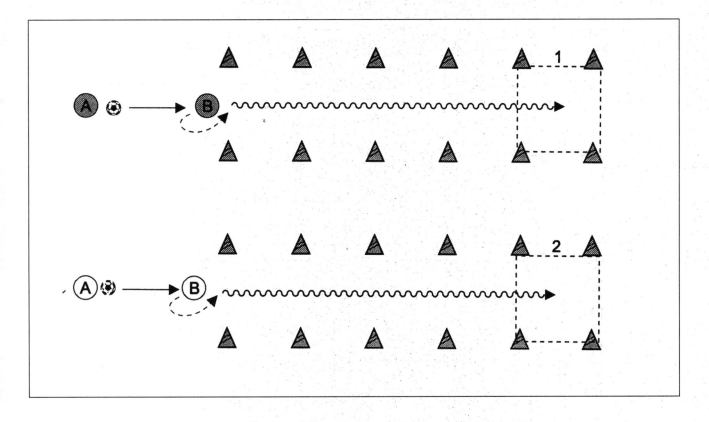

Player B receives a pass from player A, controls the ball, directs it into the straight track marked out by two parallel lines of cones and dribbles it along the track up to square no. 1 or 2.
The game is played in pairs; knock-out competition.

DRILL 4
Summary table to record and evaluate athletes' performances

Evaluation / Players	1st Test	2nd Test	3rd Test
	date:	date:	date:
	no. of passes	no. of passes	no. of passes
1			
2			
3			
4			
5			
6			
7			
8			
9			
10			
11			
12			
13			
14			
15			
16			
17			
18			
19			
20			

DRILL 4

Title:
Juggling and controlling competition in pairs

General goal:
Combining basic motor skills

Specific goal:
Enhancing juggling and controlling skills

Description:

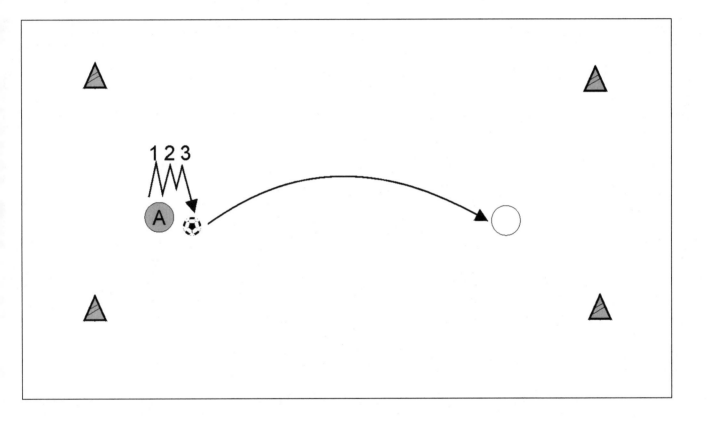

One ball for each pair of players.
Two players are standing facing each other in a rectangular playing area: player A juggles the ball three times and then passes the ball to his teammate B, who controls it without letting it bounce on the ground, juggles the ball three times and passes it back to A.
How many passes can they make without letting the ball fall on the ground?

THIRD LEVEL DRILLS

This chapter includes all the third level drills that can be used to achieve the goals previously set for the third age group (that is for 10 year old players).

Since the difficulty level of these exercises is obviously higher, the player needs to perfectly master all the basic skills and movements he has gradually acquired and enhanced in the previous games since they will be applied to real game situations involving 1 v 1 situations or competitions between small groups of players. This means that the following drills will involve direct contact and competition between two or more opponents challenging each other.

Two pages providing the coach with special directions are dedicated to each drill: the first page shows a practical summary table that the coach can use to record both objective information and his subjective notes so as to monitor his athletes' performances; while the second page includes the title of the drill, both the general and the specific goal that the exercise intends to pursue as well as the description of the game combined with the field diagram.

Only when the player has perfectly acquired and internalized basic motor skills like controlling, juggling, dribbling and kicking the ball can the coach suggest a number of basic games that obviously lay the bases for the structuring and development of more complex and well-organized play situations. All the drills I am going to show you in this chapter share a common feature: the presence of an opponent.

DRILL 1
Summary table to record and evaluate athletes' performances

Evaluation / Players	1st Test date: results	2nd Test date: results	3rd Test date: results
1			
2			
3			
4			
5			
6			
7			
8			
9			
10			
11			
12			
13			
14			
15			
16			
17			
18			
19			
20			

DRILL 1

Title:
1 v 1 knock-out competition

General goal:
Offensive and defensive individual tactical skills

Specific goal:
Playing 1 v 1 situations

Description:

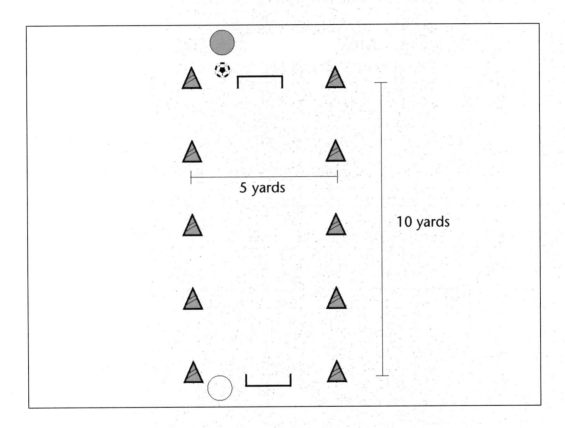

Divide the team in two groups of two players each.
One ball for each pair of players.
The two players compete against each other in a 10 by 5 yard playing area, with two goals 2 yards wide at the two opposite sides.
Each pair of players repeat the exercise ten times; the player who can score more goals directly "eliminates" his teammate.
Draw up the final results of all the various 1 v 1 situations for each team.

DRILL 2
Summary table to record and evaluate athletes' performances

Evaluation / Players	1st Test	2nd Test	3rd Test
	date:	date:	date:
	score	score	score
1			
2			
3			
4			
5			
6			
7			
8			
9			
10			
11			
12			
13			
14			
15			
16			
17			
18			
19			
20			

DRILL 2

Title:
1 v 1 situation for ball possession

General goal:
Offensive and defensive individual tactical skills

Specific goal:
Playing 1 v 1 situations

Description:

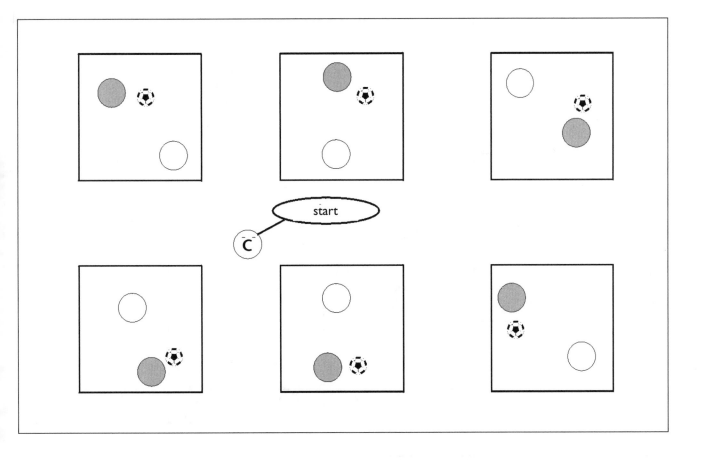

When the coach gives the starting signal, players ● try to maintain possession of the ball preventing players ○ from touching their balls and kicking them out of their playing squares. The player ● who can maintain possession of the ball longer than his teammates wins the competition.
The winner of each competition is awarded one point.

DRILL 3
Summary table to record and evaluate athletes' performances

Evaluation / Players	1st Test date: score	2nd Test date: score	3rd Test date: score
1			
2			
3			
4			
5			
6			
7			
8			
9			
10			
11			
12			
13			
14			
15			
16			
17			
18			
19			
20			

DRILL 3

Title:
Hunters and foxes

General goal:
Offensive and defensive individual tactical skills

Specific goal:
Playing 1 v 1 situations

Description:

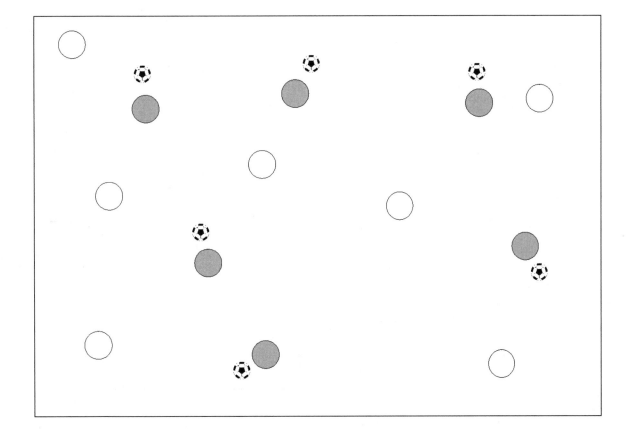

The foxes ● are in possession of the ball.
The hunters ○ play to challenge the foxes ● and kick their balls out of the playing field.
One point is awarded to the fox who can maintain possession of the ball longer than his teammates.

DRILL 4
Summary table to record and evaluate athletes' performances

Evaluation / Players	1st Test date: score	2nd Test date: score	3rd Test date: score
1			
2			
3			
4			
5			
6			
7			
8			
9			
10			
11			
12			
13			
14			
15			
16			
17			
18			
19			
20			

DRILL 4

Title:
Ball into the target area

General goal:
Offensive and defensive individual tactical skills

Specific goal:
Playing 1 v 1 situations

Description:

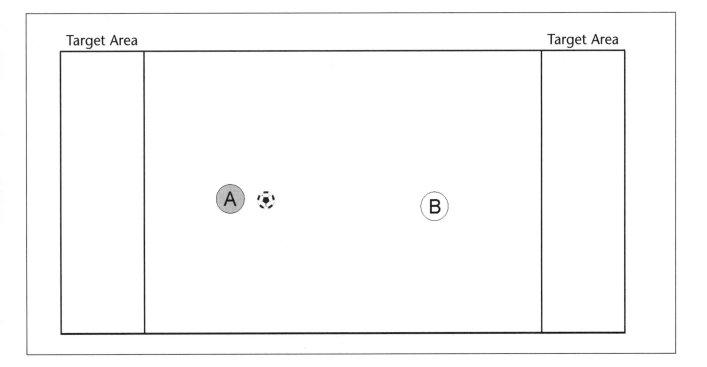

Divide the field in three zones: two target areas at the two opposite sides and a central playing area.
Player A is in possession of the ball and tries to dribble the ball into the opposite target area, beating his opponent B who challenges him.
This 1 v 1 situation is repeated 5 times; one point is awarded every time player A manages to dribble the ball up to the target area.
Player B challenges his opponent A and tries to kick his ball out of the playing field.

DRILL 5
Summary table to record and evaluate athletes' performances

Evaluation / Players	1st Test	2nd Test	3rd Test
	date:	date:	date:
	score	score	score
1			
2			
3			
4			
5			
6			
7			
8			
9			
10			
11			
12			
13			
14			
15			
16			
17			
18			
19			
20			

DRILL 5

Title:
Ball into the island

General goal:
Offensive and defensive individual tactical skills

Specific goal:
Playing 1 v 1 situations

Description:

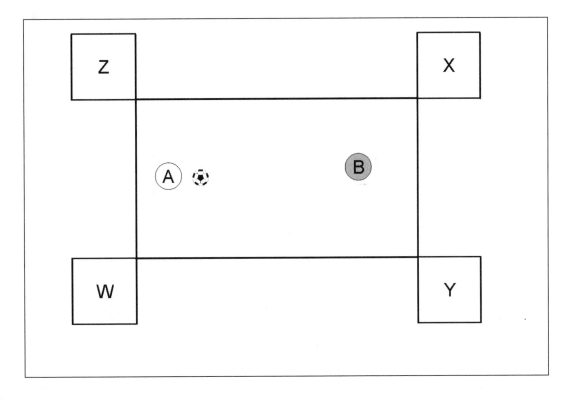

Player A dribbles the ball into one of the two islands X or Y where he stops it, while player B has to dribble the ball into one of the two opposite islands Z or W.
This 1 v 1 situation is repeated 10 times; one point is awarded every time a player manages to get into the island.

DRILL 6
Summary table to record and evaluate athletes' performances

Players / Coaching Notes	1st Test date:			2nd Test date:			3rd Test date:		
	loses the ball	wins possession of the ball	scores	loses the ball	wins possession of the ball	scores	loses the ball	wins possession of the ball	scores
1									
2									
3									
4									
5									
6									
7									
8									
9									
10									
11									
12									
13									
14									
15									
16									
17									
18									
19									
20									

DRILL 6

Title:
Playing chess

General goal:
Coaching team tactical skills

Specific goal:
Cooperation with ones teammates

Description:

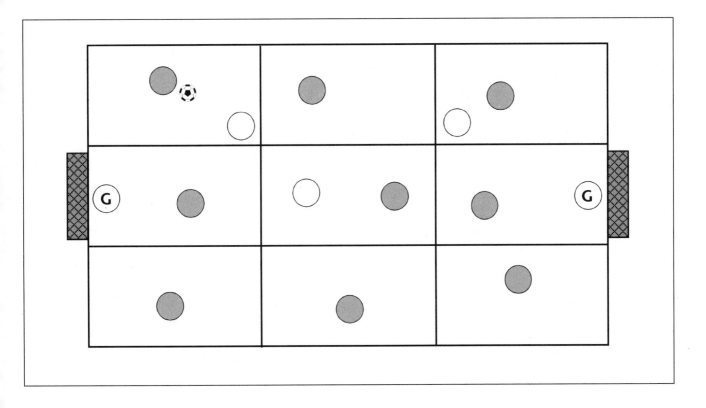

Divide one half of the playing field in 9 parts.
One attacking player in each zone and one defender every three zones.
The attacking players ● try to score a goal passing the ball to each other without moving out of their own zones, while the defenders ○ play to prevent their opponents from shooting at goal.

DRILL 7
Summary table to record and evaluate athletes' performances

Coaching Notes / Players	1st Test date:			2nd Test date:			3rd Test date:		
	loses the ball	wins possession of the ball	scores	loses the ball	wins possession of the ball	scores	loses the ball	wins possession of the ball	scores
1									
2									
3									
4									
5									
6									
7									
8									
9									
10									
11									
12									
13									
14									
15									
16									
17									
18									
19									
20									

DRILL 7

Title:
The corridors

General goal:
Coaching team tactical skills

Specific goal:
Cooperation with one's teammates

Description:

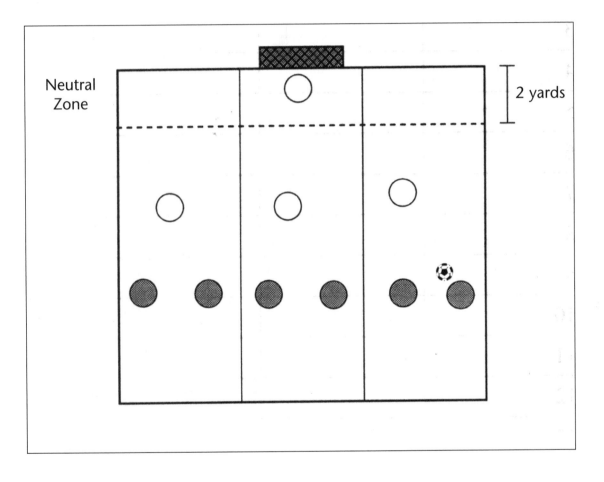

Divide one fourth of the regular playing field in three vertical zones (the corridors) and mark out a neutral horizontal lane 2 yards wide in front of the goal. Two attacking players ● and one defender ○ position in each vertical zone.
The three defenders try to hinder the offensive action of their opponents by winning possession of the ball and kicking it out of the field.
No player can enter the neutral zone.

DRILL 8
Summary table to record and evaluate athletes' performances

Evaluation / Players	1st Test	2nd Test	3rd Test
	date:	date:	date:
	score	score	score
1			
2			
3			
4			
5			
6			
7			
8			
9			
10			
11			
12			
13			
14			
15			
16			
17			
18			
19			
20			

DRILL 8

Title:
Dribble to the target area

General goal:
Coaching team tactical skills

Specific goal:
Playing 2v1 situations

Description:

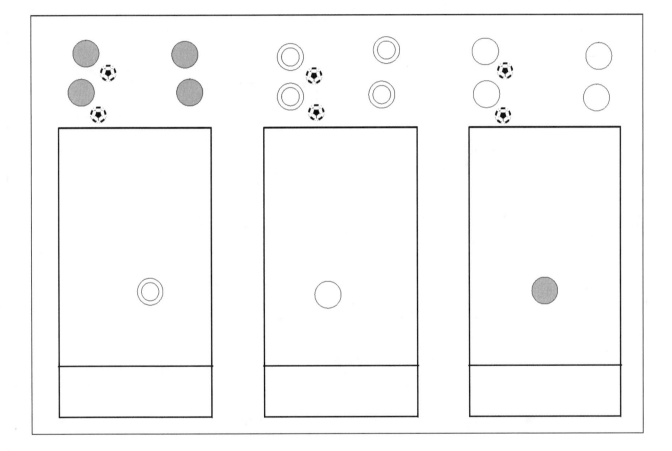

Two players in possession of the ball play to dribble the ball up into the target area, avoiding the challenge by the defender.

If the defender can touch the ball, he takes the place of the attacking player who has made the mistake, while the attacker becomes the defender.

The attackers are awarded one point every time they manage to dribble the ball into the target area.

DRILL 9
Summary table to record and evaluate athletes' performances

Evaluation / Players	1st Test	2nd Test	3rd Test
	date:	date:	date:
	score	score	score
1			
2			
3			
4			
5			
6			
7			
8			
9			
10			
11			
12			
13			
14			
15			
16			
17			
18			
19			
20			

DRILL 9

Title:
2 v 1 situation

General goal:
Coaching team tactical skills

Specific goal:
Playing 2 v 1 situations

Description:

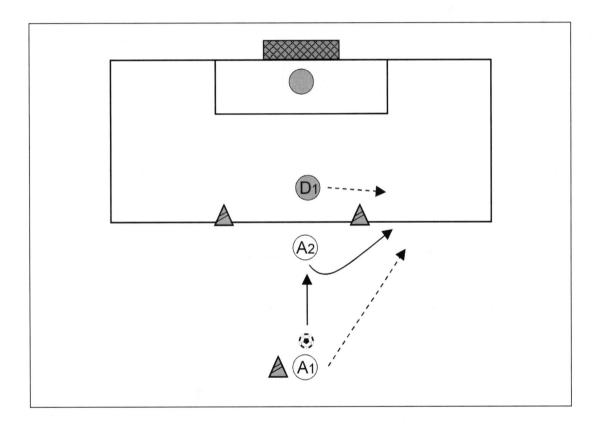

Divide the team in small groups of three players each.
Player A1 passes the ball to his teammate A2, who controls the ball, turns about and runs to shoot at goal with the support of his teammate A1, eluding the defensive action by their opponent D1.
The pair of attacking players are awarded one point for each goal they score.
If they cannot score, the defender is awarded one point and the attacking player who has made the mistake immediately replaces the defender.
Each group of players repeats the exercise ten times.

DRILL 10
Summary table to record and evaluate athletes' performances

Evaluation / Players	1st Test date: score	2nd Test date: score	3rd Test date: score
1			
2			
3			
4			
5			
6			
7			
8			
9			
10			
11			
12			
13			
14			
15			
16			
17			
18			
19			
20			

DRILL 10

Title:
4 v 4 situation with 4 goals

General goal:
Coaching team tactical skills

Specific goal:
Ball possession

Description:

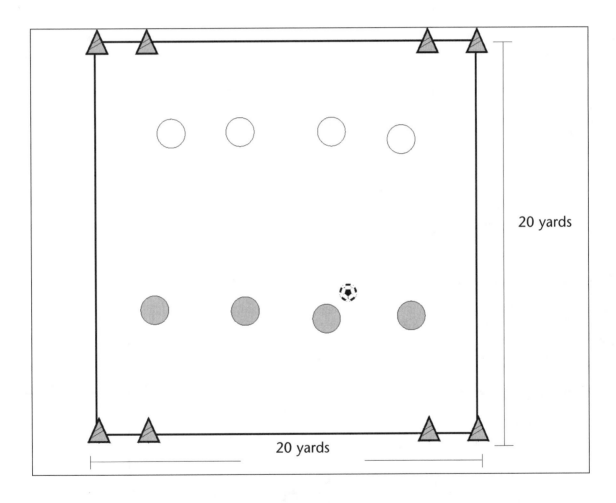

4 v 4 unconditioned game on a square playing field 20 yards wide with 4 goals, one at each corner of the field.
When a team manages to score a goal they are awarded a number of points equal to the number of passes they have made before shooting at goal.

DRILL 11
Summary table to record and evaluate athletes' performances

Evaluation / Players	1st Test	2nd Test	3rd Test
	date:	date:	date:
	score	score	score
1			
2			
3			
4			
5			
6			
7			
8			
9			
10			
11			
12			
13			
14			
15			
16			
17			
18			
19			
20			

DRILL 11

Title:
5 passes

General goal:
Coaching team tactical skills

Specific goal:
Ball possession

Description:

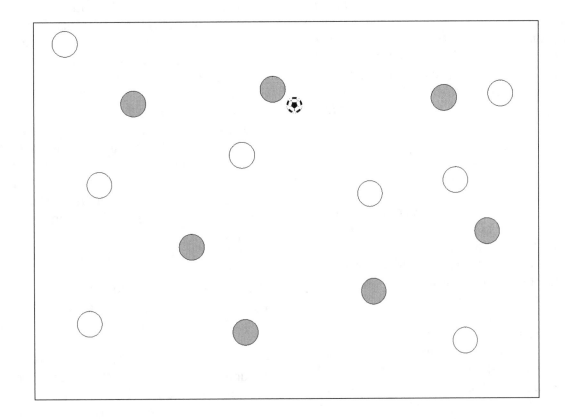

7 v 7 conditioned game on a square playing area 40 yards wide: both teams try to maintain possession of the ball making five consecutive passes, avoiding the intervention by the opposition. They are awarded one point if they can make five consecutive passes without the opponents winning possession of the ball.

CONCLUSIONS

Making a player tackle a problem that he cannot solve, simply because he is still unable to do it, intrinsically, is not an educational task, but a really cruel discouraging and humiliating experience that will certainly lead the individual to eventually give it up. It is obvious that no personality can be shaped with no effort; but only those efforts that can be and are really successful and also involve pleasure despite hard work can have an educational intent. Even hard work and fatigue can involve pleasure, especially when fatigue is completely rewarded when the individual's efforts finally bear fruit; otherwise, there is only hard work and fatigue clashing with tough obstacles where emotions and intelligence inevitably sink.

by A. Agazzi

Soccer coaches - as well as coaches or educators in general - are so often tempted not to respect, and therefore neglect, the personality of those whom they are faced with, thus imposing their own times, behavioral patterns and personal ideas. They - and I also include myself in this category - generally expect strict and stereotyped replies to their attempts to offer whatever they can and possibly more; sometimes, they are even satisfied when their athletes imitate their own behaviors as if they acted mechanically, repeating the same things like parrots.

When we are giving our coaching sessions, we may often think that we have chosen the best way and method to exploit the individual virtues and skills of one of our players simply because he replies to our inputs with accurate movements and perfect technical abilities. In most cases, we cannot realize that this is probably simply our own right method. Maybe it is the quickest and easiest way to achieve the final result. In this way, we unconsciously clip the wings of the individual's personal creativeness and originality of his motor replies, forgetting that both creativeness and originality are key in soccer.

When the coach goes to the practice field to give his coaching session, he should always remember that his job goes far beyond his planning, controlling, suggesting and directing the activity, since he is also responsible for training and educating every single athlete according to his own potential abilities.

This innovative coaching method that we have gradually built and suggested up to now clearly points out that the coach should first offer something unique and original; this is exactly the coach's job and duty: consequently, we can never forget that the person whom we are dealing with may become a very good player, but only at the right time.

While dealing with the possibility of successfully exploiting the individual's potential, the Italian author Leo Buscaglia wrote a really nice and meaningful story in one of his best-selling books "Life, love and mutual understanding":
"A rabbit, a bird, a fish, a squirrel, a duck and many others once decided to open a school. They all started to plan the program.
The rabbit obviously wanted to include running in the school plan.
The bird wanted to include flying.
The fish expected it to include swimming.
The squirrel obviously wanted the program to include climbing trees.
All the other animals also expected the school program to include their own peculiar skills, so that original plan embraced everything possible and they made the big mistake to expect all the animals to regularly attend those courses.
The rabbit could run magnificently; no other animal could run as it did. Nevertheless, the other animals said that it would be an excellent intellectual and emotional discipline to teach the rabbit how to fly and therefore said "fly, rabbit!". The poor rabbit jumped down trying to fly, and fell to the ground, breaking one of his legs. His leg was damaged forever so that he could never run so fast as he could before. So, he only got a fairly good mark for his running skills instead of an excellent one and just got a pass mark for its flying abilities thanks to his efforts.

The committee that passed the school program were all very satisfied with their choices.

The little bird also had the same destiny........ he could fly like an arrow and make such wonderful evolutions that he obviously deserved an excellent mark. But his fellow animals expected him to dig holes in the ground like a groundhog. He inevitably broke his wings and his beak so that he could no longer fly. Nevertheless, the committee were all very happy to give him a fairly good mark for his flying abilities and so forth. Do you know which animal got the best marks in the whole class? A mentally retarded eel, since he could handle any situation and apply different skills as best he could. The wise owl was terribly indignant and flew away and is now against any kind of school."

By contrast, the innovative educational coaching method we have gradually built and suggested up to now heartily encourages us to shape a truly unique and original personality. Once again I would like to remind you that the young person you are dealing with could also become a great player, but only at the right time!

While working in a school in Como I once found an official document on "The rights of children in sport", drawn up by the psychologist Dr Lucio Bizzini, the pediatrician Dr Jost Schnyder and Mr. Richard Ferrero, an expert dealing with young athletes. I take the liberty of sharing that paper with you because I think it can really help coaches reflect on their (or better, our) important role and job of educators.

The rights of children in sport:

■ the right to enjoy oneself and play
■ the right to practice sport
■ the right to play in a healthy environment
■ the right to be treated with dignity
■ the right to deal with and be trained by highly competent persons
■ the right to practice according to one's own capacities and rhythms
■ the right to compete with youths having similar possibilities to achieve success
■ the right to take part in competitions that are right for one's age
■ the right to practice one's sports discipline in a condition of total safety and security
■ the right to have suitable recovery pauses
■ the right not to be a champion.

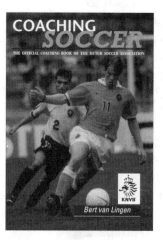

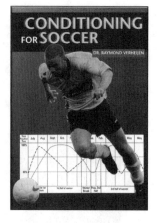

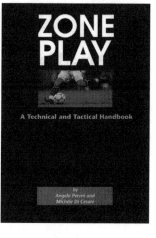

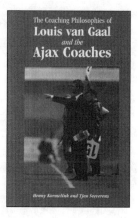
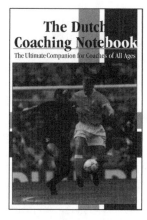

Coaching Books from REEDSWAIN

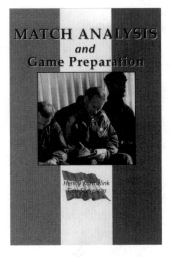
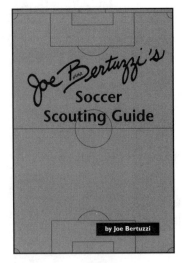
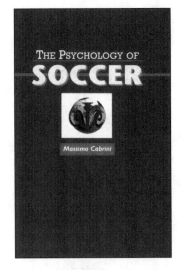